HELP THEM PULL THEIR PANTS UP

GOD BLESS!

Gilbert A. Knowles

HELP THEM PULL THEIR PANTS UP

Gilbert A. Knowles

iUniverse, Inc.
New York Bloomington Shanghai

Help Them Pull Their Pants Up

iUniverse books may be ordered through booksellers or by contacting:

iUniverse
1663 Liberty Drive
Bloomington, IN 47403
www.iuniverse.com
1-800-Authors (1-800-288-4677)

Because of the dynamic nature of the Internet, any Web addresses or links contained in this book may have changed since publication and may no longer be valid.

The views expressed in this work are solely those of the author and do not necessarily reflect the views of the publisher, and the publisher hereby disclaims any responsibility for them.

The advice and recommendations in this book cannot guarantee successful mentoring. Best practices and mentoring experiences of the author and contributors are provided to inspire, encourage, and motivate others to become involved in effective mentoring. The views expressed in this work are solely those of the author's experiences and do not necessarily reflect the views of any individuals, organizations, and institutions mentioned in this book.

ISBN: 978-0-595-50216-5 (pbk)
ISBN: 978-0-595-49903-8 (cloth)
ISBN: 978-0-595-61418-9 (ebk)

Printed in the United States of America

Contents

PART I

THE PREAMBLE

PART II

COURSES OF ACTION

ACKNOWLEDGMENTS

First, I thank almighty God for life, health, and strength. He has truly led and inspired me to write this book. Second, I thank my wife Carolyn for thirty years of marriage and friendship. She is my very best friend, with whom I share my innermost thoughts, victories, frustrations, and setbacks. She finally motivated me to put pen to paper. She also wrote the final chapter, "Develop a TIMplate for Life!" Carolyn is a retired U.S. Army officer. She served as an assistant professor of business, as well as director of the Learning Community Program (a first-year student program) at Saint Augustine's College, Raleigh, NC. Throughout her career, she has spent many years providing mentoring and educational out-reach services.

Working with Carolyn can be excruciatingly painful. She is definitely the taskmaster in this relationship. Carolyn is extremely goal and timeline sensi-tive, believing that one should write goals, create objectives, and adhere to strict timelines to accomplish the mission. As time went by, I began to fall behind on my strict timeline. Of course, Carolyn brought this to my attention. She was adamant about my not extending this timeline. Her nickname for me is "Big Attitude" because when she offers feedback and/or advice, all I give her is attitude. I guess if Big Attitude had listened to "The Warden" (what I call her behind her back), I would have been writing my second book by now. She is truly the love of my life.

The other love of my life is our only child, Summer. She is beautiful, smart, ambitious, feisty, loving, caring, and independent (until, of course, she runs a few bucks short). She calls me "Big Stress" because she says I always become too stressed, particularly when it comes to getting into her personal business. Unknowing to her, she too inspired me to write this book.

As a college senior, she called me one day, somewhat frustrated, saying, "Dad, you have to be careful with whom you share your dreams." At the time, she was a broadcast journalism major at the University of North Carolina-Chapel Hill, and she shared with some of her classmates her dream of becoming the next

Oprah. Apparently, they started giggling, as if to say "yeah, right." She declared that giggling classmates would not deter her dream. After one year of TV news reporting in a very small market, Summer was hired in a top twenty-five market. I am confident that she will be able to live her dream. You go, baby girl!

I acknowledge my independent, strong, and loving eighty-year-old mother, Alice Knowles; my beloved aunt, Alva McLeod, a retired U.S. Army lieutenant colonel, who inspired me to join the military; and my sister, Gilda Knowles, who served as one of the first reviewers of this book. I thank Dr. Mabel Jones Matthews for providing the foreword to this book and mentoring Carolyn and me for many years. I acknowledge my boss, Aaron R. Andrews, President and CEO of the United Negro College Fund Special Programs Corporation, who provided me with the opportunity to work for a nonprofit that serves minority students.

Shout-outs are given to my friend Clarence T. Brown and Cedric Greene, the designer of the front cover of this book and also the subliminally pictured graduate on the cover. I acknowledge my high school best friend, Kenneth "Falfa" Rolle. He and I engage in profound discussions, as well as small talk, almost every day. He too has contributed a major part of his adult life to mentoring minority youth.

I acknowledge my alma mater—Saint Augustine's College, Raleigh, North Carolina—for providing the start of my professional life. This place accepted me with open arms. This is where I was appointed as student representative to the board of trustees and later elected as student body president. This is where I met my college sweetheart, and now wife, Carolyn (Miss Saint Augustine's College, 1977). This is the place I discovered Alpha Phi Alpha Fraternity, Incorporated. This is where I graduated with honors and was commissioned a U.S. Army second lieutenant. This is where I returned eighteen years later to become professor of military science, later becoming dean of students and vice president for student affairs. As you can see, I have a long history with my alma mater. I will always be proud of Saint Augustine's College.

I pay tribute to all the young brothers I have worked with over the past thirty years. By allowing me to share their experiences—good and bad—these brothers have prepared me to offer the advice and direction contained in this book. The up-close lessons I have learned far outweigh any formal sociological study or social work degree. I truly cherish their friendships.

These guys definitely have my best interests at heart and many times mentor me through my frustrations, setbacks, and shortcomings. They have a raw innocence. They tell me truths not tainted by society's political correctness, deceit, lies, and betrayals. These young brothers are the sons I never had.

Finally, I acknowledge all mentors throughout America. These unheralded warriors serve in the trenches on the front lines of our communities, unselfishly working to lead young brothers in a positive direction. Very seldom are they subjects of local media reports. They just do what they have to do.

FOREWORD
By Mabel Jones Matthews, EdD

The greatest good you can do for another is not just to
share your riches, but to reveal to him his own.

—Benjamin Disraeli

My treasured friend Gilbert has a heart of gold, the faith of Job, the wisdom of Solomon, and the courage of Joseph—all of which he willingly shares with all whom he touches. His riches are built on a committed Christian foundation that is the core of Gilbert's "moral self-discipline." It is this unique richness that he shares with each of his mentees as he strives to address the needs of today's African American men.

The title, *Help Them Pull Their Pants Up*, and the content therein is a true reflection of the passion Gilbert has to tackle what he terms the American Tragedy. He has an innate ability to connect with young men, particularly of African American descent. They trust and respect him, as evident through testimonials from several of his mentees.

My philosophical view of mentoring is a professional activity that is a trusted relationship anchored in meaningful commitment. Having a close relationship with Gilbert for more than thirty years, as a colleague and friend, I have observed that our mentoring philosophies complement each other quite well. We believe that mentoring is a mutually beneficial relationship where the mentor and mentee openly share social, spiritual, professional, and personal values. It is through this openness that trust is created and outstanding breakthroughs and accomplishments are achieved, such as those featured in this book.

As a tool to aid mentors and aspiring mentors in their support of young African American men, this book provides motivation, samples of successful outcomes, and a unique approach to addressing a societal threat: the destruction of the African American male. This threat of the past ten to fifteen years, which continues to intensify each year, has the potential to eradicate a generation of young men who often appear to be rooted in negative behaviors and activities. This book will inspire you to get up, get out, and get involved! *Together* we can *Help Them Pull Their Pants Up.*

PART I

THE PREAMBLE

*"He never gave up on me
and I know I have taken him through hell!
And he never backed down along the way."*
**Abdual Lindsey
President and CEO
JerZ Media Productions
Raleigh, NC**

INTRODUCTION

But the LORD said to Samuel, "Do not consider his appearance or his height, for I have rejected him. The LORD does not look at the things man looks at. Man looks at the outward appearance, but the LORD looks at the heart."
1 Samuel 16:7
(Holy Bible, NIV)

You see them all the time, their pants hung low and underwear showing. They have tattoos on their arms and chests. They wear do-rags, caps on backwards, huge chain necklaces, and diamond stud earrings. They are seen handcuffed on the late-night news, loudly cursing on street corners, pursuing women at the malls, selling and using drugs, and lying dead in the streets. These images branded in our psyches are of young African American males. They are the six-hundred-pound gorillas in America's living rooms. We can no longer ignore the indiscretions of these young brothers.

As the media repeatedly bombards us with negative images, we could possibly perceive that all young African American males fall in one or more of these categories. To provide proper balance to this perception, I must emphasize the great personal, social, and professional achievements of many young brothers. You will rarely see these positive and productive brothers on the late-breaking news. I would like to acknowledge the many brave young brothers who have served, and are now serving in our country's armed forces. I also honor the memories of those who have given their lives in the service of their country.

Due to the preponderance of negativity, great numbers of Americans identify only with the young brothers on the late-night news. Many Americans have grown tired of the youthful indiscretions of these young brothers, demanding that the black community do something about them. Some communities have even sought legislation that prohibits wearing low-hanging pants, desperately seeking to change a misguided culture.

This is not a black community problem! I repeat: this is not a black community problem … but an American tragedy. In one way or another, Americans—various corporate and media executives, the black community, the young brothers themselves, and others in one way or the other—have fed into this problem. I beseech all Americans to overcome their resentment of these young brothers' indiscretions and accept some measure of responsibility, so that we can collectively work to solve one of America's greatest tragedies.

I too have become frustrated with the plight of the young African American male, so much so that I was guilty of a wrong approach. The initial title of this book was Pull Your Pants Up and Man Up! However, as I thought about it, the tone of this title paralleled the message many "fed up" Americans convey—the message that falls on deaf ears. Therefore, I decided to change the title to reflect the same message, but with a different tone: *Help Them Pull Their Pants Up.*

This title is used literally and figuratively. Many young brothers literally need to pull their pants up, but there are also many who figuratively need help in pulling up their academic, personal, social, financial, spiritual, and professional pants. After years of personally mentoring and talking with other mentors, I have concluded that the overwhelming majority of young brothers really want to live productive and positive lives. However, in many cases just don't know how. We should place a lot of focus on those brothers who really want help in pulling their pants up. My friend and mentee Clarence T. Brown calls them "willing vessels," those willing to make a positive change. The young African American male harvest may be plentiful, but the laborers in the field are few. Therefore, we must develop creative strategies that reach the masses. I dream of one day appearing on Oprah's show with my willing vessels, discussing the power of mentoring relationships.

There are some who believe that we should write off an entire generation and start over with elementary school aged brothers. I am of the opinion that we can not afford to write off an entire generation. We must develop strategies to salvage those brothers who want help in pulling their pants up and then ally ourselves with them to positively prepare the next generation. Although some parts of this book relate to young brothers of all ages, it really focuses on the teenage and twenty-something brothers who with the proper education, exposure and mentorship can achieve their fullest potentials. If left unchecked, this so called lost generation can negatively affect the lives of our elementary and middle school brothers.

This book is strongly recommended for young brothers, young sisters, parents, and families; churches and community organizations; K–12 and college educators; law enforcement and political officials; and mentors and communities at large. This book proposes that we stop the never-ending rhetoric and aggressively act. It stresses the fact that we have had enough think tanks ... We now need "do tanks." We have had enough hip-hop summits; we have talked ourselves to death. We have had enough community forums ... The village needs to mobilize! In essence, we must talk the talk, but more importantly, walk the walk.

I want this book to be a short and easy read, reaching all levels of our society. If you are looking for long detailed chapters with endless statistics and fifty-cent (big) words, you are reading the wrong book. My aim is to succinctly provide recommended courses of action that will possibly serve as a catalyst for realistic and sustained national dialogue on the subject. Ultimately, my prayer and hope is for this dialogue to inspire and motivate all kinds of people to participate in efforts that will *Help Them Pull Their Pants Up.*

CHAPTER 1

An American Tragedy

I beseech all Americans to overcome their resentment of these young brothers'
indiscretions and accept some measure of responsibility, so that we can col-
lectively work to solve one of America's greatest tragedies.
—Gilbert A. Knowles
Author of *Help Them Pull Their Pants Up*

Each day, we witness great tragedies, mostly in our urban areas. Too many young brothers are walking misguided paths to total destruction. Unfortunately, as they walk this path, they fall victim to poverty, unemployment, and failure. Earlier, I established that this is not a black community problem, but an American tragedy. I have chosen to focus on possible approaches and solutions, rather than the tragedy itself. Although there are other contributors to America's problems, I have specifically chosen to address the positive development of young brothers.

There are many reasons that all Americans should want to embark on this positive development journey:

- The unemployment rate for young African American men is over twice the rate of young white, Hispanic and Asian men.[1]

- Over twenty-percent of young African American men live in poverty compared to 18% of Hispanic, 12% of Asian and 10% of white men.[1]

---

1   Bureau of Labor statistics, 2006

- African American men represent 14% of the population of young men in the U.S., however represent over 40% of the prison population.[2]

- The percentage of young African American men in prison is nearly three times that of Hispanic men and nearly seven times that of white men.[2]

- For young African American men, more deaths are caused by homicide than any other cause.[3]

- The homicide death rate for young African American men is three times the rate for Hispanics, the population group with the next highest homicide mortality rate.[3]

- HIV is the sixth leading cause of death for young African American men.[4]

Also think about the huge number of young brothers dropping out of school, unemployed and involved with drugs. It is time for action!

I hope you are as disturbed by these statistics as I am. We need to know where we are so that we can determine where we are going. However, it is time to stop focusing on negativity. It is time to put on our "spiritual armor" and prepare for battle!

2   Bureau of Justice Statistics, 2006

3   National Vital Statistics Reports, 2006

4   Health, United States, 2005

Notes:

_____

_____

_____

_____

_____

_____

_____

_____

_____

_____

_____

_____

_____

_____

_____

_____

_____

_____

_____

CHAPTER 2

Why Listen to Me?

Why would anyone want to hear what Gil has to say?
The same effect that this man has had on my life
has also impacted the lives of many other people,
through his inherent teachings, insightful
wisdom, practical application, and
continuous guidance.

—Omar White
Owner and Operator
City 2 City Auto Sales
Richmond, VA

I have been in the mentoring business for over thirty years. In some way or another, I have mentored and/or touched the lives of hundreds of young brothers. Over the years, I have been repeatedly encouraged to write a book about mentoring young brothers, as well as engage in motivational speaking on the subject. I have the ability to connect almost instantaneously with these young men. My secret is simple: I never forsake my values ... I am who I am. Although in some circles my approach may seem unorthodox, these brothers are able to sense a genuine interest in their welfare. They like me to "keep it real."

I am a retired U.S. Army lieutenant colonel, former professor of military science at two historically black colleges and universities (HBCUs), former HBCU dean of students, and vice president of student affairs. I am presently director of the Division of Community and Education at the United Negro College Fund Special Programs Corporation.

Please do not think that all these brothers once wore their pants hung low; this would have been the furthest thing from their minds. As earlier mentioned, *Help Them Pull Their Pants Up* is used literally and figuratively. There are young brothers out there who literally need to pull their pants up—those who totally lack any type of proper mentoring and teaching. I have also worked with young brothers who figuratively needed help in pulling their personal and professional pants up to achieve their fullest potential. The commonality of both is that deep down inside, they desire to learn and live in positive and productive ways.

Later in this book, I will introduce you to TIM. An acronym for *trust, inspire,* and *motivate,* TIM is the reason I have achieved great success. An effective mentor must first earn trust. Once trust is established, it opens the door to inspire a mentee to achieve his fullest potential. Once he is inspired, it becomes easier to motivate him to achieve his life's goals.

This chapter is the longest. Therefore, I request that you commit yourself to detailed reading, as I challenge you to identify common threads of these ten testimonials from a random sampling of mentees. In focusing on these testimonials, please zoom in on the relationship that each has with his mentor, identifying perceptions, first impressions, approaches, and other commonalities. I then ask that you compare your thoughts and common threads with the ones cited in chapter 9, Mentor, Mentor, Mentor!

At the beginning of some chapters, you will find quotes from these young brothers. One brother in particular, Abdual (testimonial 1 and pictured opposite the introductory page), is quoted and mentioned many times because he was by far my most challenging. He was as tough a mentoring challenge as you will ever encounter. Our relationship is definitely one for the books.

These young brothers come from various backgrounds. However, you will find that their uncollaborated testimonials highlight common threads, which will assist in sewing the tears in the American fabric. Throughout these testimonials, they will either refer to me as Dean, Colonel, or Gil. I reason to guess that some of these brothers will remind you of young brothers you are presently mentoring or interested in mentoring.

TESTIMONIAL I

The first testimonial is from my toughest mentoring challenge. Abdual was born into poverty and was pretty much raised on the streets of Camden, New Jersey. You name it, and he has done it. Man, we have had many struggles over the years. The brother was so hardheaded. Through arguments, disagreements, disappointments, and triumphs, this young brother and I have weathered the storm. Over the past few years, I have witnessed Abdual's remarkable transformation. I think he's finally got it! Unbelievably, in some ways, Abdual has now begun mentoring and teaching me about the thought processes of millenials or Generation Y. This young brother, in his unorthodox way, has begun inspiring and motivating me, at age fifty-three, to live to my fullest potential. We talk at least two or three times a week. He calls me "Pops." He is the son I never had.

TO WHOM IT MAY CONCERN:

I met Dean Knowles in 1997 on the campus of Saint Augustine's College, Raleigh, North Carolina. I was sitting on the steps of the Hunter Administration Building, just minding my business. I saw a big black man coming out of the building, and he walks up to me, asking how I was doing. I said, "I'm cool. How are you?" The first thing he asked me was what I was doing with all that gold.

First thing I thought was, Who is this dude? I was fresh out of the city, not caring about anyone. Initially, I took offense, but circumstance would have it, I answered because he seemed genuinely concerned. I answered, "I just like gold!" I had three gold fronts (on my teeth) and three gold rings.

My first thought was, This guy has balls! He was called Colonel. Upon his retirement from the army, the school hired him as the new dean of students. Therefore, we started calling him Dean. I'd seen him around before, interacting with other students, yelling at people, and telling them to get off the grass. He asked where I was from and I told him Camden, New Jersey. He then invited me to his office. When he tells the story, he says I told him that I wear the gold teeth and gold rings because it makes me feel good about myself, but of course he is exaggerating. I think as he gets older, he tends to add something to the story every year.

When I entered his office, I was amazed at his accomplishments. I saw at least twenty-five to thirty plaques, mostly military associated (including pictures of him with President Bill Clinton and General Colin Powell) and one plaque about Alpha Phi Alpha Fraternity, Incorporated.

We talked about where I was from and what I was majoring in. He wanted to know my plan for success. Did I have one? And so I told him my goal was to come to college because where I'm from, there were not too many options, and I wanted to be different from the people in my family. So I explained to him that I was there to pursue a business degree, and he asked other questions about my background and things of that nature.

I can't really remember everything we discussed that day. However, I perceived that this big, loud man had a genuine interest in my well-being, which was different from what I was accustomed to from people his age. Man, he was so loud that I really thought he had a hearing aid or something.

Then I remember asking him questions about him because I was tired of him getting into my business. The first one was about Alpha Phi Alpha Fraternity, Incorporated. I had heard other students talking about what fraternity they were going to pledge, and that their relatives were in this fraternity or the other. His response was, "Do you have what it takes to be an Alpha man?" I asked, "What does it take?" He told me manly deeds, scholarship, and love for all mankind. I don't think he realizes what kind of impact he had on me when he described what it took to be an Alpha man. By the way, I am now an Alpha man.

As he was talking to me, he helped me to grab hold of a better picture of what I wanted to accomplish in life. Quite honestly, now that I think about it, he was the first real example of a true good black man who lived the American dream. It was evident in the way he dressed, presented himself, and spoke. He showed great character and, without question, belonged in a class by himself.

As time went on, we began to grow close, and from that point forward, he was constantly putting his foot up my butt! Without ever verbalizing it, he became my mentor, and I became his mentee. And just like any other relationship, we've had our bumps and bruises and arguments. I am young and know it all, and he is old and never wrong. But like any true relationship, through the fire, we were able to withstand any weapon formed against us. The enemy will always attempt to keep you from what God has in store for you. As the years passed, he became more than a mentor. He became my big brother and then a father figure.

I can truly say that for the last ten years, he has single-handedly inspired and molded my character into what it is today. I am truly grateful for him because I believe our meeting was divine, as I was headed down a road of destruction. And although I had always been eager to learn, up until then I had never had a true and good example.

He never gave up on me, and I know I have taken him through hell! And he never backed down along the way. I don't let anyone talk to me the way he does, and no one knows as much about me as he does. I know that our meeting was ordained by God. If I had to go to battle, he would be the guy I would want backing me up. I have even told him that when he gets old, I will be there to change his diaper. He immediately replied with a sarcastic statement that I won't repeat. But seriously, I really meant it.

He is the first man that I ever told I loved, and he taught me everything. It's very difficult for me to put everything that he has done for me in words. I just hope that someone will read this and be inspired or gain hope that God will place someone in his life to be a guide on how to achieve manhood so that he can "man up" and take on that responsibility, as I now do.

All his mentees talk about what they will do for Dean when they make it big. He repeatedly says that the only thing he wants from us is to reach back and help another young brother. However, with me it is different. He says that he wants me to pay back sixty dollars he loaned me in Baltimore when I was shooting kind of bad. After he took me to lunch and gave me a pep talk, we walked to an ATM, and he withdrew sixty dollars and gave it to me. His version describes it as a loan; my version is that he gave it to me. I have never met someone who possesses so much pride yet so selfless.

Although he will never admit it, I take pride in believing that I am his closest mentee. I do know that I am the one who has taken him through the most hell. Actually, I am now his son and he is my father. Whether this very proud man accepts it or not, I am forever indebted to him.

Sincerely,

Abdual Lindsey
President and CEO
JerZ Media Productions
Raleigh, NC

Notes:

TESTIMONIAL II

Omar was the "pretty boy," a curly-headed bad boy type with a keen entrepreneurial spirit. Raised in Richmond, Virginia, he also had pretty much done it all. Of all my willing vessels, he had the most "mouth." He was always ready to challenge me at every angle. He took pride in standing up to me, when others seemed intimidated. He always pursued ways of making a buck. His favorite pastime was taking photographs (mostly of women) and then selling them. He was known by the women as the cute photographer. I think they would let him take their pictures just so they could get close to him. Today, he is a great husband, father, and business owner.

TO WHOM IT MAY CONCERN:

I am writing this letter for the purpose of providing my personal testimony of the impact and influence that brother Gilbert Knowles has had on my life. I say "brother" because, as members of Alpha Phi Alpha Fraternity, Inc., a fraternal bond connects Gilbert and me, but that is not where our bond began.

Our first meeting, you can say, was on "coincidental purpose." Mr. Knowles, then Lieutenant Colonel Knowles, was the professor of military science (PMS) of the Saint Augustine's College and Shaw University Army ROTC program. He was looking down from his second-story office, which peered over the sidewalk that I just so happened to be walking on that day. He yelled out to me like an insane man and instructed me to pull my pants up. I had just gotten my ear pierced, which was a fashion statement, and he adamantly stressed to remove the earring.

My first thought was, this guy is going to be trouble. The next time I'll walk a different way. I really didn't know how to take this guy at first, but I soon learned that he was genuine and straightforward. Needless to say, I joined the ROTC program that semester, and years later was commissioned as a second lieutenant in the U.S. Army. I eventually became a captain in the U.S. Army Reserves.

Colonel Knowles adopted me as one of his many sons on campus. I wasn't an angel in school, nor did I back down to opposition. I was willing to go toe-to-toe with anyone. So I've had my share of run-ins, bumps, and bruises. Once you have survived the streets, being on a college campus seemed like a walk in the park, I thought. In the back of my mind, I wanted a fresh start, but my guard stayed up, just in case. Gil was a lot like me. He didn't back down either. On many occasions, we have squared off with differences of opinion.

I saw something familiar in him, and he cared. He was a guy that you really didn't want to disappoint. He was able to penetrate my guard and open my mind to some different possibilities and thought processes. Through the mischievousness and growing pains, he remained a one true constant throughout my college career ... and not because he was the PMS of the ROTC program.

Shortly after I joined the program, he retired and was selected as the dean of students. He was consistent in checking up on me and offering sometimes needed but unwanted advice. I drew comfort in knowing I could count on him if I needed to, and on a few occasions, he had to answer the call. He has always been comfortable correcting you in public, but at the same time, had no problem displaying publicly his love and affection for his wife, who also taught on campus. He is well respected amongst his peers and mine. I consider him the measure of a true man, a mentor, and a good friend.

Gil possesses the qualities, skill sets, and attributes needed to mentor just about any group of people, but especially youth. His personality is huge. He has a way of infecting you with his passion for being upright, straightforward, and genuine. He won't back down on his principles but respects the opinions of others. He invites challenges, shortcomings, and imperfections for the purpose of overcoming, refining, and perfecting them.

"Why would anyone want to hear what Gil has to say?" you ask. The same effect that this man has had on my life has also impacted the lives of many other people, through his inherent teachings, insightful wisdom, practical application, and continuous guidance.

When people look back over Gil's life, they won't remember how big his house was or how nice the car he drove was. They will remember how he touched and affected their lives ... and in Gil's case, they'll have a lot to talk about. He doesn't just talk the talk; he lives it!

Sincerely,

Omar J. White
Owner and Operator
City 2 City Auto Sales
Richmond, VA

Notes:

_____

_____

_____

_____

_____

_____

_____

_____

_____

_____

_____

_____

_____

_____

_____

_____

_____

TESTIMONIAL III

I first met Tyrone as a recently discharged soldier enrolling in the college's Army ROTC program. He was a little older than many of the ROTC cadets. This young brother and I have maintained a great relationship over the years. Tyrone married his college sweetheart. A couple of years ago, Carolyn and I proudly attended their housewarming. Tyrone even called me while transporting his wife to the hospital for the birth of their beautiful daughter. He is a great husband and father.

TO WHOM IT MAY CONCERN:

I consider writing this testimonial for the forthcoming book by Mr. Gilbert Knowles an honor and privilege. I met the colonel in the fall of 1995, when I transferred to Saint Augustine's College in Raleigh, North Carolina, and enrolled in the ROTC program. From the front door of the ROTC building, I could hear him disciplining a cadet. When someone told me the loud voice was the colonel's, part of me said, "I am getting out of ROTC if he starts tripping."

Once in his office, this massively built man stood up to shake my hand, and I quaked for just a second. My first impression of the colonel was that he was going above and beyond to motivate the cadets we had in the program at the time. In later years I realized he was truly being himself and was passionate about the well-being of young people.

In this day and time, many young men are raised without fathers. I was fortunate in that I had my father in my life for thirty-six years, until March of 2007. Long before my father's sudden passing, I had already started nurturing this relationship that would fill that void in my life.

I met the colonel as a young twenty-four-year-old recently divorced boy walking in a prideful spirit. He let me tell my story, and he has been walking with me every day since. He has been involved in every major life decision I have made since we met. Whether I agree with his direction or not, it is important to my growth as a man.

Smart people surround themselves with brighter people and should always have someone who can hold them accountable. My wife knows that if I start slipping in any area, the colonel is only a phone call away. He has made himself available to us in that capacity. Most people his age do not want to be involved with young couples.

Very recently, while driving my wife to the hospital for the birth of our first child, I called the colonel. Every day we take this walk through life, mostly only doing those things necessary to pay the bills. Most people never step outside of themselves to help the greater masses. The colonel has found his passion in mentoring and writing this book, and I know firsthand that his words can change your life. Turn the page; a new direction in life is on the other side.

Sincerely,

Tyrone Lynn
Program Manager
Washington, D.C.

Notes:

_____

_____

_____

_____

_____

_____

_____

_____

_____

_____

_____

_____

_____

_____

_____

_____

_____

_____

_____

TESTIMONIAL IV

Jerome, from Washington, D.C., always knew where he wanted to go. He had great spirituality and always stubbornly pursued his life's passion. He was definitely a leader. I fondly remember him influencing a group of young brothers to practice celibacy. I have no doubt Jerome remained celibate until marriage. I laughed to myself when hearing these young brothers reciting their abstinence vows. Of course, their lust eventually prevailed, but at least they put forth an effort. I also recall one night being called at home by campus security. Jerome was leading a protest against the library closing too early during finals. I remember our college president remarking that this was the kind of protest any president would like to have. The next day, the library hours were extended. Jerome is now a happily married pastor. He is also a loving father and successful entrepreneur.

TO WHOM IT MAY CONCERN:

Gilbert Knowles has been instrumental in the lives of many young African American men. Personally, Gilbert "Dean" Knowles has been a consultant and a mentor to me. He has always encouraged me to follow my dreams. When I was a student at St Augustine's College, Dean Knowles helped me get adjusted to college life without losing focus, and he was instrumental in my success.

When I arrived at St. Aug, Dean Knowles was one of the first administrators that I met, and immediately I knew he was a man of distinction, integrity, and character. He told me that I could achieve my goals, and that I would be successful. He monitored my success by having numerous meetings with me. This all paid off. I am now a pastor of a great church (Vision International Church), owner of rental properties in Raleigh and Clayton, North Carolina, owner of a production company, a husband, a father, and a servant to my community.

I would not have been able to do any of this without the Holy Spirit and the encouraging words of this great man. Dean Knowles is a great man, father, husband, and leader, not just in the community, but the world. I love Dean Knowles, and I know that he is just getting started on his quest to change the lives of as many people as he can.

Sincerely,

Jerome Gay, Jr.
Pastor
Raleigh, NC

Notes:

_____

_____

_____

_____

_____

_____

_____

_____

_____

_____

_____

_____

_____

_____

_____

_____

_____

_____

TESTIMONIAL V

Quincy, from Wilson, North Carolina, was a tough nut to crack. Man, this brother had a trigger temper and deep paranoia. He always thought someone was out to get him or confront him about something. Quincy has overcome many obstacles, and I am proud to say that he is now a happily married man and loving father. We had not seen each other for years. In speaking with him recently, I laughed at his present concern about when his eight-year-old daughter becomes a teenager. I am now counseling him in advance on what to expect when that time comes. I am so proud of him.

TO WHOM IT MAY CONCERN:

My first puff of marijuana was given to me on my eighth birthday; I chased it with some gin and honestly loved it. That would probably explain my disinterest in school at the time. While being left in a car as a child, I witnessed the repeated stabbing of a woman. You can couple this with a later experience of going on a heist and ending up in a police station. Later, my peers would say things like, "Hey, my mother said I can't play with you" or the most memorable taunt: "Dirty Lucas." I often acted out in elementary school.

My grandmother, a gift from God, raised me. When my grandmother died, I went into a deep, deep depression. I sometimes wished that somebody, anybody, would violate me enough to give me a reason to retaliate. Believe it or not, pretty soon I graduated high school and decided to pursue a college education, which was a promise I made to my grandmother. My first day at St Augustine's College was a mixture of excitement and nervousness. There were all types of people: weirdoes and geniuses … and some were a mixture of both.

One day some guys and I were sitting on the steps of the Hunter Building discussing girls; that's putting it delicate. This guy comes out of the building, and he is gigantic and very loud, and he is heading our way. Everybody looks at each other as if to say, "Okay, this guy is big, but we really don't need any extras in our conversation." This big guy walks over and introduces himself. "Hi gentlemen, I am Dean Knowles, and I hope y'all are not disrespecting my girls." I replied something like, "Nah, we are not disrespecting them, but we got plans for them." At this point, everybody is laughing, and then Dean asks me my name, in which I reply, "My name is Quincy." Dean looks at me and says, "I am going to remember you, sir!"

That was my first encounter with Colonel Knowles, and honestly, after our initial meeting on the steps, I thought I would never see him again. I didn't see any reason why I should think Dean was any different from other adults I had met.

I was completely wrong about Dean Knowles. Dean was totally different and extremely accessible. Anytime I needed Dean, he was there. Some guys felt that Dean didn't respect them, because of his abrasiveness, but I think that it was just their egos. I knew that everything Dean was kicking to me was for the betterment of my situation, and this is why I never felt that he was disrespecting me, although I did wonder sometimes what drove his behavior.

I soon learned that Dean was from Liberty City, a part of Miami, Florida. Here we have an ex soldier who is from a very serious part of Florida. This guy knows no other way to be but aggressive. Dean was always trying to get the best out of all the students he met and for that I am personally grateful.

I recall stepping in to see Dean at least twice a week. Maybe I needed a pep talk, or maybe I needed to stop by and play some new song that I felt was groundbreaking. You see, good people, this is a friend, someone who doesn't always agree with you, but someone who always agrees to listen—that's Dean.

I salute you!

Your friend,

Quincy "Q" Lucas
Screenwriter
Raleigh, NC

Notes:

_____

_____

_____

_____

_____

_____

_____

_____

_____

_____

_____

_____

_____

_____

_____

_____

_____

_____

TESTIMONIAL VI

McLaurin, from Laurenburg, North Carolina, was always a respectful, competitive, and thoughtful young brother. I remember recommending that he marry his high school sweetheart immediately after graduation and commissioning as a U.S. Army second lieutenant. He took my advice. McLaurin is now a major in the U.S. Army and happily married with two children.

TO WHOM IT MAY CONCERN:

I am writing this letter for the mere fact that without Lieutenant Colonel (retired) Knowles, my military career, along with many of my professional traits, would not have been noticed. He has shown me how to act, think, and walk among the best.

The real reason for my sincere gratitude to LTC Knowles is based on the best advice he gave me one day, which has my life filled with happiness and joy. He asked me what my plans were for my girlfriend (Sharon) when I graduated and went on to the U.S. Army Officer Basic Course. I said she would stay home and wait for my return. He then stated, "You and Sharon have been together for a long time, and she has been there for you on numerous occasions." He then asked, "Do you love her?" I replied, "yes." He said, "Then why not marry her and take her with you?" I took his advice, and twelve years later, my family is my life, and his advice and guidance were a major part of this.

When I met LTC Knowles fourteen years ago on the campus of Saint Augustine's College, I would have never thought that if I didn't have a father, this is who I would have called Dad. He has made a tremendous impact on my life. He knew from the start that I had all the qualities to be a great army officer.

Our ROTC program was a combination of two schools. The primary host was Saint Augustine's College, with Shaw University being the second school. I was a student at Shaw, and in the battalion, the commander was always from the host school. LTC Knowles gave me the opportunity to be the first ROTC battalion commander outside of the host school. This is where our daily contact and mentorship as a future army officer and son began.

There was not a day where I could leave my A-game home, which in the long run taught me that you should always have your A-game. One day I was in a room full of people, and I began telling him why I had to leave his meeting early. I stated that I had to leave because I needed to have my car's "Cadillac converter" replaced.

If you know LTC Knowles, he gives you "the look" when you have said something profoundly improper. He asked, "You're going to get what replaced?" I'm thinking to myself that this isn't an enunciation or pronunciation problem, so I said it again, this time timidly. He then asked, "What is a Cadillac converter?" At this point, I'm thinking he doesn't know much about cars; therefore, I went on to explain. From the look on his face, I knew he was setting me up for an attack. He replied, "The proper words are catalytic converter." He was not laughing, but I, to this day, think it is one of the funniest episodes I have ever encountered. If you could see some of the expressions on his face, you would also laugh.

This is the type of personal character trait he possesses. He would help you, and you would enjoy the help or would not hesitate to listen to his feedback. My peers have all mentioned how LTC Knowles has made such an impact on their lives. For me, his advice on how to support your family and always put them first, and everything else would take care of itself, stands firm. So, if you are a family man, young officer, or just a young man looking for some words of advice from a real community role model, LTC Knowles's testimony will surely help.

I would like to close by saying I am very thankful for everything that LTC Knowles has done for my family and me. Many people would sometimes say that giving material things is all that counts. I would not give up any of the guidance, advice, or mentorship that he has given me; between his teachings and those of my father, I am a true man today, which has shown me how to be a husband, father, and role model in the African American community.

Sincerely,

Mondrey O. McLaurin
Major, U.S. Army

Notes:

_____

_____

_____

_____

_____

_____

_____

_____

_____

_____

_____

_____

_____

_____

_____

_____

_____

TESTIMONIAL VII

I sometimes called Quinton my "quiet storm." Born and raised in Washington, D.C, he was somewhat quiet. However, when provoked, he could quickly become an erupting volcano. This great young brother has a heart of gold, and he is the type who takes friendships very seriously. He will always have your back. Quinton is now happily married and serving as a church deacon. Another willing vessel, Jerome Gay, is his pastor.

TO WHOM IT MAY CONCERN:

The brother, friend, and father figure Dean Knowles still has a great impact on my life after so many years of not hearing his voice or seeing his face. As a young man coming from the inner city streets of Washington, D.C., I had no idea that I would meet someone who cared about brothers' and sisters' well-being, but I did through Dean Knowles and his wife. They were both educators and wanted to see positive change in students.

I can recall the first day meeting Dean on the campus of Saint Augustine's College in the fall of 1997; he was a man on a mission; the man knew my name before I even knew his. He said, "Young man, how are your grades?" I said that they were okay, but I was lying, and he could tell. He kept asking questions about my goals for the school year, and what I was planning on doing with the major I had chosen. I had no clue; all I'd wanted to do was get out of the city and make a fresh start on life.

Dean was always challenging students to make better grades, take care of their hygiene, and most importantly, respect the campus grounds. I can recall mornings in the cafeteria eating breakfast with Dean; it was always a treat because he'd impart some wisdom on me and people that were around him. Even though I didn't like how it came out, it made me a better person because he was a man who talked from the heart, and if the story that you were telling him didn't sound right, he'd let you know right there. He had my ear, whether he knew it or not.

I really missed Dean when he left St. Aug at the end of my sophomore year. There was a time in my life that I needed Dean to have my back, but he had already left. It was a morning in the cafeteria, and I had an altercation with another young man during breakfast. I was suspended from school for the remainder of the year.

I came back to school focused. However, I soon got a phone call that my father had passed away. I went home to bury my father and came back to school, stayed to myself, and really got serious about living for God. Later, I made the dean's list and was so proud; I couldn't wait to one day tell Dean about my accomplishment.

That day finally came when I saw him on the campus; he said, "Sir, how are you doing in your classes?" I replied that I made the dean's list. He was so proud of me because I stuck to the plan. I went on to graduate with a business degree.

I currently serve as a deacon at my church, and I am married to a beautiful woman of God. I thank God for sending a man who was so real and who cared about making a difference in young people's lives. Keep doing your thing, Dean!

Much love,

Quinton Armstrong
Deacon
Raleigh, NC

Notes:

_____

_____

_____

_____

_____

_____

_____

_____

_____

_____

_____

_____

_____

_____

_____

_____

_____

TESTIMONIAL VIII

Rodrick, from Alcolu, South Carolina, has always been a superstar. He was always the poster boy for success. He graduated with honors from Saint Augustine's College; was selected as a Fulbright Scholar; earned a Harvard graduate degree; and is now a vice president for International Economic Development in a major city. Rodrick was recently chosen as one of *Ebony* magazine's 2008 "America's Future Leaders." Rodrick is the type of young brother everyone wants to mentor. Therefore, he has many mentors he can always call upon. The college president even chose to mentor him. Over the years, Rodrick has continued to nurture these relationships. He is happily married and the father of two children.

TO WHOM IT MAY CONCERN:

I'm writing this letter to provide a firsthand testimonial regarding Gilbert Knowles—my mentor, friend, and big brother. I first met the colonel as a gangly senior in high school considering Saint Augustine's College on an ROTC scholarship. The first thing I thought when I met him was, Whoa! This guy is intense. I don't know if I can take four years of this. I also thought, I really like him. He seems like someone I can trust.

Although I did not attend St. Aug on an ROTC scholarship, I got to know Colonel Knowles well over the next four years. I was St. Aug's superstar. Everyone, including faculty, always lauded me for my scholastic, professional, and personal achievements. He applauded me as well, but equally reminded me of how I could improve, and what I needed to do to be the absolute best.

His uncompromising expectation of near perfection was what I needed to push me from being just a good student to being a really great person. The colonel was just as concerned about my personal well-being and commitment to my value system, as he was about my being a good student. His commitment to excellence and belief in the power of the individual are apparent to all who know him. He has an unsettling ability to assess a person quickly—his integrity, character, and will. He then provides pointed direction, guidance, and big-brotherly advice or admonition, if needed.

As he is an imposing figure in size and personality, one must listen to what he has to say. His advice is always balanced, well thought out, and motivational. I will never forget his favorite phrase, "BAB—Be about business!" A career serviceman, his character is unquestionable, and his work ethic shines through in all he does. I'm writing this letter because I know the impact that he has had on my life and the lives of many of my friends. He is not one who just talks. He leads by example.

...u supported my application for a graduate degree at
...ter of fact, he wrote one of my recommendation letters. I suc-
...s endeavor and am now a vice president of International Economic
...ment.

...n closing, Gilbert Knowles has the ability to reach young men in a way that few can. His ability to relate to the urban condition, combined with his mix of tough love and genuine concern about community, rings true.

Sincerely,

Rodrick T. Miller
Vice President
International Economic Development
Phoenix, AZ

Notes:

_____

_____

_____

_____

_____

_____

_____

_____

_____

_____

_____

_____

_____

_____

_____

_____

_____

_____

TESTIMONIAL IX

Clarence, hailing from Augusta, Georgia, was in his middle thirties when we met. He is the one who applied the term "willing vessels" for those wanting help in pulling their pants up. He is also the author of *Radical Introductions* and *Raising a Radical Child*. He is a spirit-filled brother with a great desire to make a difference in life. We are comfortable in sharing our innermost thoughts, frustrations, and triumphs. He too is happily married and the father of a great son.

TO WHOM IT MAY CONCERN:

Let me tell you a little story about a man named Gil. The retired lieutenant colonel just loves to keep it real. Then one day when I was looking for advice, he offered it to me and it wasn't very nice.

But it was true, a reality check of sorts. What can I say about Gilbert A. Knowles that nobody knows? Probably nothing. If you are reading his book, you will see many testimonies, anecdotal evidences, and golden nuggets that reveal the truth about this man.

Gil will tell you that he has hundreds of young brothers. Some I know, and some I do not. But none of that has prompted me to write this letter. I write this letter from one "old head" that he helped not too many years ago. In life, there are few chance meetings that actually shape your life in such a way that they alter your existence. But when they do happen, they are big. This is exactly what happened between Gil and me.

When I first met Gil, it was at a conference in Baltimore, Maryland. His presence was overpowering, his words were distinct, and his actions were distinguished. He so impressed me that I just had to find out more about this man. He invited me to sit with him for breakfast one morning, and we talked briefly, but that left me even more intrigued.

I saw so much of myself in him that it was scary. The defining moment came when I tried to give him my business card. He looked at me and said, "I don't want that. I have hundreds of them in my desk. If you want to stay in contact with me, it is on you." Now that was brutal honesty, and I liked it. So many others will and have taken my card and never thought about it again, but not Gil. Now, I was a grown man working at a professional job, with a family, but there was something about him that made me feel like a student sitting at the feet of the master.

I e-mailed Gil weeks later, thanking him for his hospitality and requesting an opportunity to come and visit with him. Without a second thought, he agreed to it, and in another week, I was on my way from North Carolina to Virginia. Gil and I sat and talked for a couple of hours, and he dissected me as only a true surgeon can. He asked questions of me, which caused me to open my life like a book.

Gil listened carefully to everything I had to say and then asked for my resume. Once I acquired it and shared it with him, he ripped into me with reckless abandonment. I can still hear his words as if it were this morning. "What have you done with the last four years of your life?" he asked. As I tried to justify my complacency, he delved further: "Don't you know that you just have six months left on your job at best?" he retorted.

The federal grant that provided me employment was due to end in about six months. The truth was that until that moment, I had not given it much thought. That barrage of questions started moving me toward my true potential. As I left Gil's office that day, I knew that he was right, and that I needed to do something about the blinders that I had been wearing. Over the next couple of weeks, I sat down and wrote out a complex plan that included detailed goals for the next six months of my life.

Within two months of our meeting, my life had done a 180-degree turnaround. Soon after visiting Virginia, I returned for a job interview with Gil's corporation. The funny thing is that the only thought that I had about the process was that I did not want to embarrass myself in front of this man. But once it was over, I was hired, and our relationship intensified. Gil became my resident mentor.

During the past three and a half years, we have shared many laughs, tears, accomplishments, and setbacks together. We share each other's faith, visions, goals, inspirations, and aspirations.

Today, I can truly say that I have become a better man because of that meeting one fateful day in Baltimore. Today, I can say that Gil has grown beyond being a mentor; he is a big brother, a confidant, and a *friend*. I just pray that one day I can look back over my life and say, "I have hundreds of little brothers/sons" and know that they feel the same way about me that I feel about Mr. Gilbert A. Knowles.

Sincerely,

Clarence T. Brown
Program Manager
Fairfax, VA

Notes:

_____

_____

_____

_____

_____

_____

_____

_____

_____

_____

_____

_____

_____

_____

_____

_____

_____

TESTIMONIAL X

Nicholas, from Brooklyn, New York, is a smart, well-spoken, and polished young brother. We have not known each other for very long. However, it seems as if we've known each other for a lifetime. This "Morehouse (only all male HBCU) man," chosen in 2005 as one of *Ebony* magazine's "America's 30 Future Leaders," is a class act. On Christmas Eve of 2006, he proposed to his future wife on the top of the Eiffel Tower. They had a great wedding and honeymooned in Greece. By the way, he married a "Spelman (one of only two all women HBCUs) woman" who is an excellent lawyer.

Dear Gil,

I consider it both an honor and a privilege to have been asked to contribute my thoughts about mentoring to your book. It is clear to me that you have devoted your entire career to mentoring others, and I am proud to have been adopted by you as one of your "sons." Our society faces a critical shortage of quality role models. I am constantly inspired by the fact that you have chosen to serve while many others have turned and run in fear from our young people.

According to the National Mentoring Partnership, mentoring is a "… trusting relationship that brings young people together with caring individuals who offer guidance, support and encouragement aimed at developing the competence and character of the mentee." Though we have known each other for less than a year, you are the person who makes me think most frequently about the value and commitment of mentors. So often our young people believe that no one cares if they live or die. So often their dreams are deferred because they have no one to help nurture them. So often are their cries for help ignored because the older generation doesn't understand the new language of youth–or the generations in between are too focused on "getting paid."

Throughout my life I have been blessed to be adopted by many mentors. Even before I had embraced community service as a career and a way of life, several of my elders saw something in me that frequently I couldn't see for myself. They encouraged me to plan ahead, work hard, and persevere through difficult situations. They taught me that "good enough" is never a way to conduct business; that if it was worth doing it was worth doing well. My mentors have been men and women, much older than me and close to my age, of different ethnicities, economic backgrounds, and career paths. Some were in my life only for a short time; others will be with me until death parts us. My mentors taught me many lessons, but the one that stands out as most important is that investments made in people yield the highest returns.

Gil, in the relatively short time we have known each other, I have been continually inspired and motivated by you. You move with purpose, almost single-minded in your desire to help young men realize their stifled potential. You push young people toward their personal best because you know that sometimes you are the only one who expects them (us) to achieve. You set a standard that is far above what most young men come into contact with–a standard that major media outlets don't want to admit actually exists in African-American communities.

In a society where you frequently find phony, self-absorbed, and self-centered "role models," it has been refreshing to connect with you and get to know you. The trust and respect that I have for you is easy because I know that you absolutely have my best interests at heart. You role model manhood in the truest form: you provide for your family emotionally, physically, and financially; you and Carolyn model a successful long-term marriage; and you make it clear that your daughter is the center of you and Carolyn's world. In all seriousness, I want to be like you when I "grow up."

In short, Gil I am glad you are in my life. Your mentoring has made it possible for me and others to be better mentors. Your friendship has made it possible for me and others to be better friends. Your light shines brightly enough to illuminate the path for those coming behind you, and I, for one, am grateful. At the risk of sounding any cheesier than I already have, I'll end this letter here. I hope that you know that the words of this letter are both true and heartfelt, but probably don't go far enough.

With love and admiration,

Nicholas M. Bassey
Program Manager
Fairfax, VA

Notes:

_____

_____

_____

_____

_____

_____

_____

_____

_____

_____

_____

_____

_____

_____

_____

_____

_____

_____

These testimonies say it all. The intent of the testimonials was not to glorify Gil, but to provide you insight to the thought processes and expectations of young brothers. Though these young brothers come from different backgrounds and experiences, the common denominator is TIM (trust, inspire, motivate), with trust being the bedrock of successful mentoring. Hopefully, you will look forward to comparing our common threads notes in chapter 9. Your threads and mine will lead to enhancing our mentoring strategies in *Helping Them Pull Their Pants Up*.

Common Threads Notes:

_____

_____

_____

_____

_____

_____

_____

_____

_____

_____

_____

_____

_____

CHAPTER 3

Prepare for Battle!

If I had to go to battle, he would be the guy I would want backing me up.
—Abdual Lindsey
President and CEO
JerZ Media Productions
Raleigh, NC

It is time to prepare for battle. The battle is for the positive development of young African American males. I think we can all agree that something must be done and soon. American will is the strongest on earth. If we put our minds to it, we can win this battle. Battles must be carefully and strategically chosen. Too many well intentioned battles have been lost due to poor execution and support. It is time for us to become conquerors and not victims.

America's population is now over three hundred million. However, only about 1 percent of the population has chosen to serve in our armed forces. This very small force is stationed throughout the world to protect us from all enemies, foreign and domestic. The Vietnam War, proven to be in direct conflict with the will of the American people, put an abrupt end to the military draft and started the all-volunteer military. The battle I propose will be no different. Mentors will not be drafted. They must want to volunteer. Unfortunately, the number of volunteer mentors will be too small to fight the traditional battle. Therefore, we must develop creative strategies to fight the enemy.

One option is to utilize what the military calls "Economy of Force." We must position our mentoring and educating forces where we get the most bang for the buck. Overwhelming forces must be strategically positioned to break through the enemy's main line of defense. Too many times, we wage battles requiring resources we do not have. We also often choose battles that do not have the total support of our communities. Sometimes it is better to win small battles and leverage these small victories to successfully fight the next.

Communities must develop realistic battle plans. America's societal battlefields are littered with young African American male casualties. Many result from self-inflicted genocide. Battles can be long and arduous, with attacks, counterattacks, flanking movements, air attacks, retreats, and major casualties. Prior to going into battle, the U.S. military conducts an "Estimate of the Situation." This estimate is used to assess strengths and weaknesses and develop effective courses of action to soundly defeat the enemy. I offer my short and altered version of a societal "Estimate of the Situation," as it pertains to young African American males.

ESTIMATE OF THE SITUATION

What is the mission?

Clearly and succinctly define your mission statement. What do you want to achieve? What is the major reason for going into battle? Is this an achievable mission? What are the potential consequences if this battle is not waged? The mission must be thoroughly analyzed. Check out an example of a mission statement:

Significantly increase the positive and productive development of young African American males through proper education and effective mentoring.

ENEMY FORCES

Once the mission is defined, you must identify potential obstacles to complete victory. Who are the enemies? An effective reconnaissance of the enemies will reveal their strengths and weaknesses. Why are these enemies so effective in our communities? Who are their allies? Let's look at some of these enemies:

Drugs are used by too many young brothers to escape the realities of life's battlefield. Born into poverty and harsh environments, they must daily face and cope with the pressures of survival. Too many young brothers also choose to sell drugs. This steady and easy cash flow affords them luxuries seen on TV. Due to lack of education and positive environments, they see no other way to enjoy the good life. They have become the piranhas in our communities.

Potential strengths of this enemy: inactive communities; school dropouts; unemployment; misguided support structures; poverty; and ignorance

Potential weaknesses of this enemy: education; strong families; strong drug prevention and rehabilitation programs; strong law enforcement; low drug demand; and total community involvement

Gangsta culture is a major enemy. This culture justifies disrespectful behavior, crime, and violence as a way to gain "street cred." Projecting toughness is essential to their survival in the hood. The perceived lack of love and attention from their families lead to joining gangs. They are looking for love and respect in all the wrong places. Gangs effectively fill this void. The gangsta rap genre perpetuates the image of low-hanging pants, fighting, and owning and sometimes using guns. It personifies the bad boy image. This is what they see, and this is what they do.

Potential strengths of this enemy: school dropouts; intimidation of community members; bad boy image; unloving and unsupportive families; fatherless homes; unemployment; gangsta rap; and inactive communities

Potential weaknesses of this enemy: loving and supportive families; community activities; church activities; athletics; strong law enforcement; effective mentoring; high school and college graduation; employment, and effective tip hotlines

Middle and high school dropout rates reflect a disinterest and dislike for formal education. Many times this results from unsupportive and weak educational home lives. Falling behind academically, these young brothers become frustrated and take what they think is the easy route. They drop out of school. The gangsta mystique persuades these young brothers that academic excellence is not cool. Many attempt to project street smarts rather than book smarts. Lacking social and professional skills, the school dropout becomes discouraged and frustrated when attempts to find (those who do attempt) employment result in failure.

Potential strengths of this enemy: no reinforcement of academic excellence at home; lack of parental support of teachers; parental inability to foster discipline in the home; frustrated, tired, and uninspired teachers, counselors and administrators; lack of school funding; and lack of mentoring

Potential weaknesses of this enemy: strong educational reinforcement at home; active parental participation in school activities; creative teaching approaches; effective mentoring; active tutoring programs; college tours; and adequate school funding

Unemployment is yet another enemy thriving off the accomplishments of the other enemies. Ironically, many young brothers look down their noses at working in food establishments. They would be totally embarrassed if their posse saw them working behind a burger counter. Too many uneducated, unskilled brothers refuse to work minimum wage jobs. Unemployment results in idle time.

Potential strengths of this enemy: school dropouts; boredom; lack of parental, family and community support; lack of discipline; poor social and professional skills; lack of hope; frustration; lack of effective mentoring; and racism

Potential weaknesses of this enemy: strong parental, family, and community support; strong and effective mentoring; social and professional skills training; employment counseling; strong schools and education; creative tutorial programs; and staying in school

Crime is a formidable enemy fed by the aforementioned enemies. The more uneducated, unemployed, gangsta culture-oriented, drug-dealing brothers we have, the more crime is conducted in our neighborhoods. What other alternatives do they have to survive? Many seem to feel more comfortable in a two to three-mile radius of their homes, resulting in local community members and businesses falling prey. A life of crime leads to high incarceration rates.

Potential strengths of this enemy: poverty; quick cash; gangsta rap; low self-esteem; unsupportive families; no-snitching culture; unemployment; and prosperity envy

Potential weaknesses of this enemy: strong community tip hotlines; employment; supportive families and communities; and strong law enforcement

Misguided sex is another powerful enemy. The lack of education, employment, and finances tends to emasculate too many young brothers. Therefore, sexual prowess becomes a true measure of a man and promotes many sexual conquests. Too many young brothers boast the number of their babies' mammas. This false sense of manhood produces lustful and unloving unions, resulting in unprepared fathers not equipped psychologically, educationally, socially, and financially to become responsible providers. Thus, single-mother households evolve, and the vicious cycle continues.

Potential strengths of this enemy: R-rated movies with strong sexual content; gangsta culture; lack of sex education; pornography; and promiscuous environments

Potential weaknesses of this enemy: abstinence; strong sex education programs; strong parental role-modeling; church attendance; and effective mentoring Check this out: Dropping out of school begets uneducated brothers; uneducated brothers beget unemployment; unemployment begets a severe lack of resources and idle time; lack of resources and idle time beget a life of crime and misguided sex; a life of crime and misguided sex begets incarceration and single-mother households.

Are we grasshoppers in our own eyes?

Can these enemies be defeated? Are we totally intimidated? Are we grasshoppers in our own eyes? There are several verses in chapter 13 of the book of Numbers (Holy Bible, NIV) that speak to the grasshopper mentality. These verses speak of the Lord telling Moses to explore the land of Canaan. The explorers found a land with milk and honey, with large, powerful, and fortified cities. A suggestion was made that they could truly take possession of this land. But, the men who had observed the large city inhabitants felt they should not attack because the inhabitants were too large and too strong. Verse 33 mentions the following: "We seemed like grasshoppers in our own eyes, and we looked the same to them."

Are we grasshoppers in our own eyes? If we believe that we are, so will we be in the sight of the enemy. Are the drugs, gangsta culture, school dropouts, unemployment, crime, misguided sex, and other potential enemies too formidable? Are we committed to the fight until the victory trumpet sounds? Should we hoist the flag of surrender before the battle starts? Should our young brothers continue down the road of destruction without our intervention? We must answer these questions before we attack the enemy. The estimate of the situation continues with determining our friendly forces.

FRIENDLY FORCES

Who are likely supporters in achieving our mission? How many warriors will we have? What support elements are required? What results do we want to achieve? Do we have the will of the people? Do we have a long-term commitment to fight the battle to its very end? How long will they be able to participate? Who will cover our flanks? Who will provide the reserves for a counterattack? Some potential friendly forces are parents, families, mentors, K–12 schools, colleges, and communities.

Parents must be at the forefront of the battle. The positive development of their sons is at stake. I feel rather guilty admitting that I considered placing parents in the enemy category because, in too many cases, parents are the root of the problem. Their earlier mistakes have come home to roost. They model the wrong behaviors that eventually show up in their sons. With all this said, I believe the majority of parents would be strong warriors because the positive development of their sons is at stake. I can't fathom parents not being involved in this battle.

Families serve as reinforcements for this battle. They must provide strong safety nets to both the young brothers and their parents. They must counterattack when the enemy has penetrated parental lines. Grandparents, particularly grandmothers, have a long history of supporting their grandsons. Uncles, aunts, and cousins must join the counterattack by providing love and support.

Mentors are the secret weapons. History has taught the enemy that communities lack strong and effective mentors and mentoring programs. Therefore, the enemy would be totally surprised to find a strong committed mentor actively involved in teaching, exposing, and educating young brothers. These secret weapons will strike a devastating blow on the enemy. Mentors will prove to be an invaluable ally.

K–12 schools, vocational schools, colleges and other alternative education programs serve as the heavy artillery in this battle. Serving as the bastions of education, they offer our sons pathways to positive, productive, and meaningful lives. Effective educational programs led by teachers, professors, counselors, and administrators will be able to fire their "educational artillery" at the enemy.

Communities provide air cover for the battlefield. Churches, community organizations, government agencies, and politicians are able to look at the entire battlefield and swoop down on the enemy when it is most vulnerable. In previous centuries, warriors wore armor to protect themselves in battle. Helmets, breastplates, shields, footwear, and swords were used to shield them from enemy attacks. Today's battle is no different. Communities must protect themselves with the whole armor of God.

SPIRITUAL WARFARE—GOD'S ARMOR

The right armor is essential in preparing for the battle of the century. Spiritual armor is undoubtedly the best protection from an unrelenting enemy. Ephesians 6:10–17 (Holy Bible, NIV) says, "Finally, be strong in the Lord and in his mighty power. Put on the full armor of God so that you can take your stand against the devil's schemes. For our struggle is not against flesh and blood, but against the rulers, against the authorities, against powers of this dark world and against the spiritual forces of evil in the heavenly realms. Therefore, put on the whole armor of God, so that when the day of evil comes, you may be able to stand your ground, and after you have done everything, to stand. Stand firm then, with the belt of truth buckled around your waist, with the breastplate of righteousness in place, and with your feet fitted with the readiness that comes from the gospel of peace. In addition to all this, take up the shield of faith, with which you can extinguish all the flaming arrows of the evil one. Take the helmet of salvation and the sword of the Spirit, which is the word of God."

COURSES OF ACTION

We have defined the mission statement and identified our enemy and friendly forces. Now is the time to provide effective courses of action to win the battle. See what you think of the following courses of action. They will be fully defined in the following chapters.

- ❖ Take Our Village Back!
- ❖ Find *That* Man!
- ❖ Conduct a Briage!
- ❖ Actualize *No* and *Busy*!
- ❖ Educate, Educate, Educate!
- ❖ Mentor, Mentor, Mentor!
- ❖ Develop a TIMplate for Life!

This estimate of the situation is used only as a guide. Like fingerprints, each community will have its own imprint and must address its own challenges.

This estimate can also be developed for individuals. What mission would you like to embark upon with your son? What are the obstacles (enemy forces) in his path? Who will be his allies (friendly forces)? What courses of action will you take to achieve your mission?

Here is a review of the estimate of the situation:

ESTIMATE OF THE SITUATION

Mission Statement

Significantly increase the positive and productive development of young African American males through proper education and effective mentorship.

Enemy Forces

    a.   Drugs

    b.   Gangsta culture

    c.   Middle and high school dropout rates

    d.   Unemployment

    e.   Crime

    f.   Misguided sex

Friendly Forces

    a.   Parents

    b.   Families

    c.   Mentors

    d.   K–12 schools and colleges

    e.   Communities

Courses of Action

    a.   Take Our Village Back!

    b.   Find *That* Man!

    c.   Conduct a Briage!

d. Actualize *No* and *Busy*!
e. Educate, Educate, Educate!
f. Mentor, Mentor, Mentor!
g. Develop a TIMplate for Life!

Notes:

_____

_____

_____

_____

_____

_____

_____

_____

_____

_____

_____

_____

_____

_____

_____

PART II

COURSES OF ACTION

CHAPTER 4

Course of Action #1
Take our Villages Back!

It takes a village to raise a child.
—African proverb

We all are familiar with the African proverb "It takes a village to raise a child." Many say this is not happening today. I disagree. Today, misguided villages are raising our children. As previously mentioned, drugs, gangsta culture, middle and high school dropout rates, unemployment, crime, and misguided sex are influencing young brothers. These enemies are raising our children as never before, leading many down the road to total destruction.

Many of our village members do nothing about the negative influences devouring our youth. These young brothers are running numbers, selling drugs, disrespecting property, fathering children, dropping out of school, stealing, maiming, and killing. How long will a tired and frustrated village tolerate these serious indiscretions? Just think: Teenagers are calling the shots in our villages. They are ruling our villages through intimidation, fear, and retaliation. We must stop blaming the White man for all of our ills. Some of our own brothers have become our oppressors and worst enemies.

Crime should be color blind. There should not be a double standard. We must show the same outrage towards Black perpetrators of crime as we do White perpetrators. Black on Black crime is horrendous. One would think that our communities give Black perpetrators a pass on crime. We as a people tend to immediately respond to a perceived racial injustice. Case in point: The Jena 6 in Louisiana. We had our self appointed leaders and scores of African

Americans from throughout the country converge on Louisiana to protest this injustice. There was such great support for the Jena 6. I ask what about the self inflicted genocide raging in our own back yards? Where is the outrage? Where are the protests? What about a national march on Washington including the many, many mothers and families who have lost their sons from black on black crime? This march could possibly spark a major backlash against perpetrators of crime in our communities.

It is time for villagers to charge out of their burglar-barred, deadbolt-locked dwellings and encounter the enemy, not with weapons, but with support, education, and mentorship. Fear is not in God's plan. Therefore, put on the whole Armor of God and attack not with weapons but a unified front of education, support, mentorship, and guidance. We have brothers killing each other over nothing, disrespecting our sisters, burglarizing our neighborhoods, and selling drugs to our children. Some of our own brothers have become our worst enemies. The village must mobilize its parents, churches, citizens, schools, and politicians. Together they comprise a formidable force.

"Can we all just get along?" This remark was made by the infamous Rodney King, the brother unmercifully beaten by the Los Angeles police. Is it possible that we can all just get along to launch a massive counterattack on the enemy? I say yes!

Message to parents: step up your game!

Parents, it is keepin' it real time. Some of you are responsible for the roots of your sons' behaviors. Your missteps and miscalculations have led to many of the problems. Too many of you are very young and still learning about life yourselves. Many of you are still out in the world having your young fun. Guess what? The party ended when your child was born. Too many of you are modeling or have modeled the same negative behaviors now displayed by your sons.

You have to promote education in your households. You have to get more involved with their school activities. If you are not educated, you need to go back to school yourselves. Granted, I know that some of you are working hard and getting tired and frustrated. However, you have to step up your game. Instead of blaming societal injustice and teachers, unite with teachers, counselors, and administrators in educating your sons. You must involve yourselves at parent-teacher conferences/meetings, monitor homework assignments, and champion superior academic performance.

When is the last time you voted? If you have voted, did you take your son with you? Have you been involved in the community? Have you gotten to know your public officials? Have you worked with local community organizations?

Have you allied yourselves with the church? Have you volunteered to help someone less fortunate? Have you gotten your son involved in community activities? Have you attempted to foster a better relationship with law enforcement? Have you taken your son to free local cultural events? Have you taught African American history to your sons? Have you told them about our struggles over the past four centuries? Have these young brothers truly digested the challenges faced by our ancestors? Do they really know about the Middle Passage and subsequent slavery? Are they familiar with Jim Crow? Do they know about the lynchings? Do they know about Emmett Till? Do they know about the church bombing that killed innocent little girls? Do they know about the water hoses and police dogs? Do they know how many people died so that they may enjoy today's freedoms and opportunities?

Single parents, have you considered group parenting? What about sharing dinner meals? What about teaming up with another single parent in buying a car for transportation to work and taking your children to school, community, and cultural activities? What about sharing the food bills? What about listening to another person's child when the parent and child are not getting along?

Sometimes we become so frustrated, tired, and confused that we don't realize that the same actions are producing the same results. No matter how strongly we think things will change, they don't. It is time to engage new strategies and approaches to fight the enemy. The only way to take our village back is to step up your parenting game!

Message to sisters: step up your game!

You are more powerful than you may think. Boys live to impress girls. Therefore, if you do not tolerate certain behaviors, young brothers will eventually adjust accordingly. Too many of you are attracted to the bad boy types. Consider checking out the young brothers who are interested in living positive, productive, and lawful lives. As African American queens and princesses, you should be treated as such.

I beseech you to never allow any of these brothers to disrespect you. I strongly recommend abstinence. However, if you choose to have sex, please, please ensure that appropriate protection is used. Do not end up like so many of our young sisters, getting pregnant by a young brother who is not equipped emotionally, financially, or psychologically to be a supportive and productive mate. Sisters, you deserve better. Step up your game!

Message to churches: step up your game!

The church has long played a pivotal role in the positive development of its people. Can we say the same today? Do you sponsor any programs for young brothers ... or is the building fund your major aim? Have you formed coalitions with other churches to make a major difference in the village? Do you have active youth ministries? Do you have tutorial programs?

Many of you are active in supporting foreign missions. Are your domestic missions equally as active? Have you lately taken a collection for activities focusing on the positive development of young brothers? Are your men actively involved in mentoring programs? Are your women involved with mentoring young mothers? Do you sponsor college days and tours? Have you teamed with local schools focusing on young brothers? Do you have walls of tradition that turn off young brothers?

In uniting with parents, community organizations, schools, law enforcement officials, and other churches, there is no doubt the enemy can be defeated. With God on our side, defeat is not an option. Please reach out to these young brothers who don't own a suit. Please educate and guide these misguided brothers. Please welcome them warmly into your sanctuaries. Please let them know that God is the only answer to their ills. The only way to take our village back is to step up your churching game!

Message to the village: step up your game!

It is time to help single mothers positively raise their sons. It is time to foster relationships with law enforcement officials and report crime and so forth. It is time to work with churches and political organizations. It is time to stand up to the teenage bullying. It is time to mobilize neighborhood watch programs. It is time to counter the anti-snitching culture.

Do you have strong after-school programs? How about a combined group mentoring effort involving representatives from churches, community organizations, schools, and law enforcement? This program would provide four to five mentors for 25 young brothers in the village. The community organizations and churches would support group activities for these young men.

These activities could include tutoring sessions, sports and social activities, nature hikes, college tours, and community service projects. Imagine: five of these groups could positively reach 125 at-risk youth. These groups would provide positive role models and enhance the sense of camaraderie among the young brothers. Periodically, all of these groups would unite for positive group activities sponsored by churches, schools, community organizations, and law enforcement.

Mothers, fathers, community organizations, churches, schools, mentors, and young brothers would be required to sign contracts specifying roles and responsibilities, as well as rules of engagement (e.g., attendance, commitment, and positive reinforcement). The camaraderie displayed among these young brothers could attract more to sign up for this positive program. Through fostering a loving family-oriented experience, this program could eventually replace gangs. We cannot take our village back unless the village steps up its game!

Message to law enforcement: Step up your game!

Community policing is a major step in taking our villages back. Too many law enforcement agencies have less-than-stellar reputations in our villages. Although some of these reputations are deserved, many are promoted by the enemy. The majority of you are good public servants committed to healthy villages.

Law enforcement officials must work harder in fostering trusting relationships with the village. Increasing trust with village members will result in more people coming forward to report crime. I recommend that you strengthen partnerships with churches, community organizations, schools, and village members to counter the no-snitching mentality.

Increasing your involvement in community activities and mentoring programs will reap great benefits in executing your mission. You must step up foot patrols in our villages. You must develop relationships with village members; ensure no unwarranted heavy-handed experiences; show that you too are members of the village; heavily emphasize the safety of tips hotlines; provide more funding for public relations campaigns and programs; and respond quickly to high-crime areas. We cannot defeat the enemy without your total involvement and commitment. You are an invaluable ally. We cannot take the village back unless you step up your game!

Message to local politicians: step up your game!

I beseech you to seek funding for the positive development of young brothers. In a later chapter, I will talk about keeping young brothers busy. The busier they are, the less time they have to be in the streets. They won't be able to be busy unless there are various village activities to consume their time. You are our leaders. Have you sought or sponsored after-school programs? How about funding for community centers?

At times, there are village perceptions that their local politicians have abandoned them. They only see you during campaign events or visiting their churches at election time. They constantly see you posing at gala events with local VIPs, but are you equally in the hood? Granted, many of these perceptions may be unwarranted. However, perceptions, right or wrong, are real to them.

Please take more time and be visible in the village. Please sponsor proposals for neighborhood community development. Please work together with local churches, schools, community organizations, and law enforcement officials in fighting the enemy. Please develop more trust in our villages. Please interact with those young brothers no one will talk to; and please listen. We cannot take our village back without your active support ... Please step up your game!

Message to brothers: step up your game!

There are so many of you achieving great and wondrous things as sons, husbands, fathers, brothers, providers, mentors, professionals, and community members. Although you are achieving great things, you can always step up your game. I request your help in delivering this message to the brothers that are shirking their responsibilities of manhood. These are the brothers not living positive and productive lives; not respecting women; not financially and emotionally supporting their children; not earning an honest and decent wage; not respecting the lives of other people; and involving themselves in lives of crime. The message to deliver: "Our people have come a long way. Our sisters have made tremendous strides personally and professionally. Quite honestly, you are the weakest link in the African American culture/community. Too many of you are taking the easy way out, dropping out of school, adding to the unemployment rolls, hanging on the corners. I say to you my brother, you can make a change. There are community members and mentors willing to provide guidance and help. Give them a chance. Please better respect our women. If you are going to have sex, please make sure you use proper protection. If you impregnate a woman, accept the shared responsibility of your child. Leave the drugs alone. Quit the life of crime. Help our people, don't oppress them. You can positively impact change...if you step up your game!"

I truly believe that the combined efforts of the entire village can lead to the total defeat of the enemy. This defeat will create a renaissance within the African American village—a village that will be inspired to create better environments for our young brothers, allowing them to achieve the American dream.

Notes:

_____

_____

_____

_____

_____

_____

_____

_____

_____

_____

_____

_____

_____

_____

_____

_____

_____

_____

CHAPTER 5

Course of Action #2
Find *That* Man!

I just hope that ... God will place someone in his life to be a guide on how to achieve manhood so that he can "man up" and take on the responsibility, as I now do.

—Abdual Lindsey
President and CEO
JerZ Media Productions
Raleigh, NC

Many young brothers reside in single-parent households, the majority headed by women.

To single mothers of brothers:

Imagine yourself as a runner in a relay race, with baton in hand, fiercely running your portion of the race. You finally reach your destination to hand the baton to a man, and he is nowhere to be found. You think to yourself maybe he will be at the next handoff point, but still no man. You are now getting tired and frustrated. However, you are keenly aware that you must continue the race—a race that has seemingly evolved into a marathon.

This analogy parallels the struggles of many single mothers of brothers. You find yourself all alone in your struggle to reach the finish line. For the sake of raising your son to become a strong, responsible man, it is imperative that you find *that* man. Not a man for you, per se, but for your son. However, if *that* man happens to be for you as well, that's even better. *That* man is strong, upright, committed, courageous, good, and genuine. *That* man will always be at his appointed place to receive the baton.

Granted, there is no earthly love stronger than your love for your children. I assume that it has something to do with you carrying this God-given creation in your womb for nine months. This is something men are obviously not equipped to do. There are also some things that you are not totally equipped to do alone, such as providing a balanced upbringing for your son. Some of you have accomplished this feat almost all alone. However, I suspect that at some time in their lives there was some strong male influence.

There is no doubt that you have a very special love for your children, but I have found that your sons have a special effect on you. The same can be said about fathers and their daughters, but let's save that for a later book. Let's specifically focus on your relationship with your sons. It is tough raising sons today. Outside negative influences are stronger than they have ever been. Therefore, boys require tough, strong men in their lives to assist in their proper and total development.

I am convinced that men are innately tougher on boys, and women tougher on girls. I suggest that, perhaps unknowingly, some of you tend to display what I call "son worshipping". He is Momma's little man. Many sorry young momma's boys become sorry men. I beseech you to find *that* man.

Recommendation #1: Don't allow your personal feelings about a failed relationship interfere with the father's involvement in his son's life.

In some cases, you will determine that it is best to keep the father out his son's life. Due to abusive, violent or criminal behavior, it may be best for him to stay out of the equation. However, I have found, in some cases, that the vengeance for the father results from hurt feelings of a failed relationship. At times, this vengeance is so strong that the father is totally released from any type of emotional or financial accountability.

This decision results in financial hardship. As we all know, two paychecks are better than one. In many cases, stubbornness leads to raising your family in a life below the poverty level. Some of you are forced to depend on public assistance or work two and sometimes three jobs to make ends meet. While you work long hours to ensure bills are paid, your sons are being raised by negative influences in the street. I strongly recommend that you resolve whatever issue(s) you have with the father and allow him in your son's life.

Notes:

_____

_____

_____

_____

_____

_____

_____

Recommendation #2: Insist that if there is no emotional connection, there darn well better be a financial one.

I can hear some of you asking, "What about the father that does not want to be involved in his son's life?" I am glad you asked. It is imperative that the father financially support his son. If his name is on the birth certificate, he is legally bound to provide some type of financial support.

Unbelievably, I have witnessed some of you feeling sorry for *sorry* fathers who whine about their financial hardships. Many have decided there will be no connection. Do not let these irresponsible fathers off the hook. Many of these so-called financially strapped fathers will go on to other relationships and father other children. I have sadly witnessed these financially strapped fathers somehow being able to provide love and financial support for these children, but not for yours. Why should taxpayers take on the financial responsibility of your child? There are legal ways to ensure that deadbeat fathers provide financial support. You must not allow them to shirk their God-given responsibility of providing for their families.

Notes:

_____

_____

_____

_____

_____

_____

_____

Recommendation #3: Realize that *that* man comes in all shapes, sizes, and colors.

When reality reveals the father is not going to be involved in his son's life, it is imperative that you find a man who will mentor your son. *That* man can fill the void in your son's life. He can be a blue- or white-collar worker. Although, I personally recommend strong African American men, *that* man can possibly be of another race. I have witnessed men of other colors make strong connections with young brothers. There is no excuse for your not having a strong male presence in your son's life. He may be found in your family—namely grandfathers, uncles, *god*fathers, and so on. He may be found at your local church, at work, or working at your local store. He may be found at one of many organizations (100 Black Men, fraternities, Urban League, NAACP, Boys & Girls Clubs, etc.). There are so many programs (mentoring, tutoring, etc.) out there. Many of these programs require mentors to submit to background checks. These checks are very important…do not allow just anyone to mentor your son. Believe it or not, there are programs that struggle with finding young brothers to mentor. There is no excuse not finding programs having strong and upright males to mentor your son. You must find where these programs are available in your cities.

Notes:

_____

_____

_____

_____

_____

_____

_____

_____

Recommendation #4: Don't be afraid to approach *that* man.

Please learn to place fear aside when approaching a potential mentor for your son. Think about the enormous opportunity that you will be providing your son when you face this fear or embarrassment. There are some cases where someone may refuse to mentor your son. Don't take this personally. He may be mentoring others or realize that he just doesn't have the time at this point in his life to become totally committed. Remember, the most successful mentoring relationships are long term. If your son projects a bad attitude that can turn off potential mentors, you may want to keep him in check.

You must be confident that someone will eventually say yes. You must keep trying. One word of caution: don't approach a mentor if there are unresolved issues with the father wanting to be more involved in his son's life. This leads to petty jealousy between the father and the mentor. The last thing your son needs is to be confused by this competition. Of course, the son will naturally gravitate to the father—a circumstance that is totally unfair to the mentor. Being human, mentors could possibly wonder why they should take time with this young brother when his father is willing and able.

Notes:

_____

_____

_____

_____

_____

_____

_____

_____

_____

Recommendation #5: Never take *that* man for granted.

I have actually witnessed some mothers attempting to use *that* man as a babysitter. Yes, I have seen mothers dropping their sons off with mentors while they go on dates or out partying. I know that many of you are young and still want to have your fun. However, don't have your fun by attempting to make *that* man a bona fide babysitter. He is spending his time and effort in developing your son to become a *that* man himself.

You, of course, have the final say in the raising of your son. But, do not sever the mentor's relationship because you perceive he is too tough. Although they may complain, boys like toughness, competition, challenges, and intrigue. Don't ever think your son can't handle tough love. It will benefit him later in life. Yes, your son will complain because he may have become accustomed to your smothering and overprotective love. Give the relationship time. In most cases you will be surprised to learn that your son is tougher than you thought and when challenged, will rise to the occasion.

Please ensure your son is never emotionally or physically abused by a mentor. Never surrender your authority, however ensure the reasons for severing the relationship are sound.

Notes:

_____

_____

_____

_____

_____

_____

_____

To mothers with fathers at home:

I constantly hear strong fathers complaining about their wives' constant intervention when it comes to them raising their sons. The mothers complain that they are too hard. I say to those mothers, *Back off!*

If you have a good and strong husband who applies a man's touch in raising your son, don't get in his way. Please remember that a father's touch is essential in raising a young brother. If there were more strong and caring fathers' touches in our families, we would not be facing the many tragedies we witness today. Unless the father is abusive, back off. Let a father do what he has to do to ensure that your son will grow to be a strong and responsible man.

Your innate desire to rescue your son from all of life's challenges doesn't allow him to grow. He must learn to endure life's challenges. You will not always be around to take care of him. I have seen this affect the marriages of young brothers. They constantly look to momma to solve their problems, rather than try to work things out with their wives. In some cases, I have found the mother has more influence over the son than the wife, causing major marital problems.

Recently, I spoke with a mother who has a strong husband attempting to help raise her son from a previous relationship. She admitted that she gets too involved when her husband attempts to provide a strong hand in his upbringing. She confessed that at times she undermines her husband in this endeavor. She said she knows her behavior is not good for her son, but she says she just can't help herself when he gives her that smile. She vowed she would make a better effort to support her husband.

I also spoke recently to a strong father who expressed his frustration with his wife's constant intervention when he is attempting to toughen up his son. She thinks he is too tough. He said his son reacts differently to his mother. He cited an example of a time his son entered the room thinking his mother was present. The son entered crying like a baby. However, when he realized the father was instead present, he immediately stopped crying. The father's presence got a stronger reaction.

Notes:

_____

_____

_____

_____

_____

_____

_____

_____

You will find *that* man's contributions will reap major benefits. Your son will learn responsible manly behavior. Over time, you will witness a remarkable transformation in attitude, strengths, actions, and successes. Please allow *that* man to help produce *that* man! Please engage others you trust in determining *that* man candidates.

Potential *that* man candidates:

_____

_____

_____

_____

_____

_____

_____

_____

_____

_____

_____

_____

_____

_____

_____

_____

_____

_____

CHAPTER 6

Course of Action #3
Conduct a Briage!

What do you think? If a man owns a hundred sheep, and one of them wanders away, will he not leave the ninety-nine on the hills and go to look for the one that wandered off?
And if he finds it, I tell you the truth, he is happier about that one sheep than about the ninety-nine that did not wander off. In the same way your Father in heaven is not willing that any of these little ones should be lost.
Matthew 18:12–14
(Holy Bible, NIV)

I struggled writing this chapter. The above bible passage provides a powerful message. In today's world, it sometimes seems as if ninety-nine brothers wandered off and only one stayed. This is my conflict: My mentoring experiences have taught me there are some brothers out there best left alone, but, the words above say you must go after all of those that wandered off.

Unfortunately, some wandering brothers are so devoured by a life of crime, gangs, drugs, and stubborn misguided mentalities that they have absolutely no desire to lead positive and productive lives. On the other hand, it is my opinion that the vast majority of young wanderers yearn for some form of mentorship. I warn that what I am about to say will be controversial. However, due to the severity of the times, coupled with a large harvest and few laborers, I suggest conducting a briage. There, I said it, a briage!

A briage is a word I made up combining brothers and triage … briage. Webster's II New Riverside Dictionary defines triage: "a process for sorting

71

injured people into groups based on their need for medical treatment." They are normally sorted in three groups: those too far gone to make it; those that will make it with help; and those who will make it with or without help.

My briage recommends a less morbid approach. I use a traffic light analogy:

1) Red Brothers. Stop! *At least for now,* do not spend too much of your limited mentoring resources on these young brothers.

2) Yellow Brothers. Proceed with caution! These brothers could go either way. Place the majority of your mentoring resources with these brothers.

3) Green Brothers. Go! These brothers will succeed with or without your help. However, they still require mentoring.

Red brothers: *stop!* These are the wanderers who do not want to be found, *at least for now.* My mentoring experience suggests that they would consume invaluable time, energy, and limited resources, which, if redistributed, could positively affect the masses. These young brothers are so devoured by the criminal culture and so stubborn in their misguided mentalities that they have absolutely no desire to make a positive change in their lives. These are the brothers who without hesitation would blow your brains out. These are the brothers who will rob an 80 year old woman and kick her when she falls. As mentioned earlier, villages must make tough and unpopular decisions as to where they will allocate limited resources.

I will not tell you which or how many brothers in your villages fall in this category. I suspect that you already know who they are. Should your limited resources be invested in those so embittered by their negative circumstances in life or by those so comfortable with their lives of crime? Should time be sacrificed for those who repeatedly refuse to accept the welcoming hands of mentors and loved ones?

Should mentors risk their safety placing themselves in dangerous criminal environments? Should mentors focus their time on those brothers whose families continually model and reinforce negative behaviors? Sometimes these young brothers have to reach rock bottom before they are willing to be found. Unfortunately, in many cases, rock bottom will be in prison or other negative life altering challenges. These brothers don't want any help in pulling their pants up because they are perfectly satisfied with their pants hung low. Some people may criticize this part of the briage. To those of you who want to place major emphasis on Red brothers, I pray God's blessings upon you succeeding.

Yellow brothers: Proceed with caution! These are the young wanderers at a crossroad.

They can go either way. The majority of these young wanderers really want to be found, but they lack the proper education, guidance, support, and mentorship required to bring them back to the flock. Your village must determine which brothers fall in this category.

Are these some of the brothers living a life of crime, but willing to make a positive change? Are these the recent school dropouts? Are these the brothers who clearly know right versus wrong, and with the proper guidance can make it through the light before it turns red? Are these the young brothers who require alternative educational options? Are these the young brothers trying to make it on minimum wage jobs? Are these the brothers seeking the proper way to live prosperous, productive and positive lives? Are these the young fathers who truly want to be good providers for their children? Are these the young brothers wanting to leave the hood? Focusing on these young brothers would reap major benefits for our villages.

Green brothers: *Go!* These young brothers will succeed regardless of whether they receive help or not. These brothers never wandered off. They stayed focused on the task at hand. They are the brothers who achieve academic excellence. For the most part, they have learned and are practicing right versus wrong. Let them go forward and do great and wondrous things.

I am not saying not to mentor these young brothers. All of them require some form of mentoring. However, I am saying that these brothers need the least amount of help. Many of them have strong and loving mothers, fathers, and families. Many of these brothers' families expose them to all types of educational opportunities. Their families model positive and strong relationships. These brothers are usually actively involved in extracurricular activities. These brothers already know that graduating from college is a given. These brothers admire their parents. These brothers know that low-hanging pants will not be tolerated.

We must reach as many willing vessels as possible. With our major focus on the Yellow brothers and to a lesser degree the Green brothers, we would have reached the masses. We can then use the talents of our Green brothers and recently converted Yellow brothers, to reach out to our Red brothers. You may have noticed that I kept saying *at least for now* for our Red brothers. I don't believe we can write off any of God's children however, it will eventually come a time when the Red brothers will want to be helped. Maybe after incarceration and other consequences from their actions they may finally want help in pulling their pants up.

Have you heard about the prodigal son? This son left home and had a pretty wild life. He eventually hit rock bottom and wanted to return home. Upon his return home, the prodigal son's father welcomed him with open arms and celebrated his return. We should always be prepared to welcome our Red brothers back home. Once they return, we must show them love and compassion.

Notes:

_____

_____

_____

_____

_____

_____

_____

CHAPTER 7

Course of Action #4
Actualize *No* and *Busy!*

Even though I didn't like how it came out, it made me a better person because he was a man who talked from the heart, and if the story that you were telling him didn't sound right, he'd let you know right there.
—Quinton Armstrong
Deacon
Raleigh, NC

No is one of the world's most powerful words. Many people have difficulty with this word. It stirs emotions, produces disappointment and creates animosity. I am of the opinion that if we used this word more often, we would not be experiencing many of the problems we face today. Saying no takes courage and discipline. Saying no sometimes creates major consequences. On the other hand, saying no can promote positive results.

If more teenage girls said no, we would not have many teenage pregnancies and subsequent consequences; if more young brothers said no more often, we would not have as many drug addicts; if they said no more often, we would not have much gang activity; if they said no more often, we would not have as much crime. As it relates to this book, the word *yes* proves to be more dangerous: "Yes, I will have sex with you," or "yes, I will join the gang."

I am no psychologist but, I would reason to guess that not wanting to say no is directly related to people wanting to be liked. No is perceived as negative, and yes is perceived as positive. Saying no usually requires an explanation. Saying no can lead to bad attitudes. Saying no can result in the silent treatment. Saying no can lead to the rolling of eyes. Parents and adults must *just say no* more often.

Many of these young brothers take the answer no as a challenge. They find it intriguing to change a young sister's no to a yes. They also like to challenge their mothers' noes, and many times are quite successful. If you want to see a mother's eyes brighten up, just mention her son's name. I beseech parents, families and mentors to say no more often. If the no is right, don't allow these cunning young brothers to change your minds.

As mentioned earlier, sometimes the word *yes* can be counterproductive to positive development. "Yes, you can do your homework later." "Yes, you can stay out a little later." "Yes, I will buy you that gangsta rap CD." "Yes, I will buy you those two-hundred-dollar sneakers." "Yes, I will tell your teacher you were sick today." Do you see how the popular word *yes* can negatively affect young brothers? It is imperative that we actualize the word *no*. It may be painful in the short term—but beneficial in the long run.

Let's now discuss the word *busy*. In an earlier chapter, I mentioned that boredom is one of the major reasons young brothers get into trouble. Boredom in the classroom results in school dropouts. After dropping out, boredom results in too much time on their hands. With too much time on their hands, boredom leads to making bad decisions.

Carolyn and I found that our daughter performed best when she was busy with extracurricular activities such as dance, karate, and track. I remember nights after track practice when she would finish her homework and want to go directly to sleep without even talking to her friends on her cell phone.

It is my opinion that guys get bored more quickly than girls; therefore, you must keep them busy. I believe all that adrenaline and testosterone leads to hyperactivity. They require an outlet. I suggest getting them involved with extracurricular activities like football, basketball, baseball, wrestling, golf, soccer, boxing, karate, and bodybuilding. I am even beginning to recommend teaching chess to brothers at an early age. Through this game, they will learn patience, as well as how to develop strategies. Can you imagine young brothers playing chess instead of hanging out on the streets?

In many cases, these brothers will enjoy the competition and camaraderie associated with these activities. They will also learn structure and discipline. There are so many programs available, and many of them free. Parents should offer no excuses for not keeping their sons busy. Granted, keeping your sons busy will also keep you busy (transporting them to the many activities, etc.), however, sacrificing the time now, will pay major dividends later—keeping them from the negative influences and temptations the streets offer. I say keep them busy until they drop!

Notes:

_____

_____

_____

_____

_____

_____

_____

_____

_____

_____

_____

_____

_____

_____

_____

_____

CHAPTER 8

Course of Action #5 Educate, Educate, Educate!

The colonel was just as concerned about my personal well-being and commitment to my value system as he was about my being a good student.

Rodrick Miller
Vice President
International Economic Development
Pheonix, AZ

Far too many young brothers drop out of public schools. As mentioned in an earlier chapter, the lack of education leads to unemployment, poverty, and crime. Therefore, education is truly the major ingredient in the positive development of young brothers.

I say let's stop pontificating about what young brothers are not doing and focus on educating them. Although our goal should be to get them back in school, in many cases we must accept the likelihood that they will not return. Due to their older ages, many dropouts feel ashamed to go back to the eighth, ninth, tenth, or eleventh grades with much younger classmates.

Let's first address keeping our sons in school. I am of the opinion that teachers get a bad rap from parents, students, and communities. Teachers are supposed to teach, however, end up spending an inordinate amount of time addressing student behavioral issues and the *personal baggage* they bring from home. Again, parents are responsible for the roots of their sons' behaviors.

If parents don't step up their games and work with teachers, counselors, and administrators, all may be for naught.

I recommend the establishment of a community-wide *"School Dropout Reaction Squad."* This squad, comprising volunteer teachers, counselors, church members, social workers, community organization members, fraternities, etc., will be immediately notified by school officials when it is apparent that a young brother has dropped out. This squad will immediately contact and visit the young brother and his family to determine the cause(s) of dropping out and help facilitate a solution for his return to school. The squad will continue to monitor the progress of these brothers.

If they are not already established, I recommend the enactment of new and creative teaching strategies, focusing on different learning styles. Case in point: My wife and I have totally different learning behaviors. She is very detailed oriented. She must read all the fine print in her learning process. I, on the other hand, just want the bottom line. I don't need the details; just provide me with the big picture.

In my acknowledgments, I mentioned that working on this book with my wife has been excruciatingly painful. During our conversations, she was extremely detail oriented. Many times I had already determined the bottom line of her conversation and did not require the minute details. To keep the peace, I would patiently await her conclusion. Unfortunately, through my well known facial expressions, she detected my impatience and then called me "Big Attitude."

I am fascinated by learning and thinking styles. Learning about these styles revealed why I do not learn well from long lectures and long-winded speakers. I enjoy and learn best from experiential and hands-on educational approaches. I wonder how many young brothers in school or those that have dropped out are more interested in this type of learning rather than reading chapter after chapter. I also wonder how many, because they weren't exposed to their ideal learning styles, felt dumb when they did not achieve academically.

RIGHT-BRAINED VERSUS LEFT-BRAINED THINKERS

Right brained thinkers tend to look at wholes (the big picture). Left-brained thinkers tend to look at parts (the details). I have learned that I am definitely a right-brained person, and my wife is left-brained. This theory says that the brain has two sides that control two different modes of thinking. People tend to favor one side or the other. However, some people are able to master both sides.

There is no doubt that I am right-brained and Carolyn, left-brained. Because I am a right-brained person, I can imagine that a left-brained teacher could drive a right-brained student crazy. If they already haven't, teachers should study this theory and provide a holistic brained approach to teaching and maintaining the interest of both sides of the brain. I wonder if many young dropouts are right-brained students being taught with left-brained teaching approaches. I suggest the readers of this book research this theory. I believe it could help in personal, social, and professional relationships.

TO COLLEGE OR NOT TO COLLEGE? THAT IS THE QUESTION

Many parents dream of their children attending college. In many cases, their sons would be first generation college graduates. Although our hopes and dreams are for our sons to get that college diploma, we must ensure that we are not setting the academically unprepared brothers up for failure. I have witnessed many parents forcing their sons to go off to colleges (that will accept them) knowing full well they were academically and attitudinally unprepared. If they made terrible grades and displayed poor study habits in high school, what made parents think they would do well in college. However, there are some that make it. At least four of the willing vessels came to college to get away from their environments. They were not the best prepared, however persevered, graduated, and now doing quite well.

We must discern those who are ready and those who are not. Those who are severely unprepared end up dropping out. The primary difference between a high school dropout and a college dropout is that the high school dropout doesn't have to pay back loans; a college dropout does.

We must pursue more realistic approaches in getting our school dropouts off the streets and off the unemployment rolls. Some young brothers are going to drop out no matter what. We must discover other safety nets for them. Let's discuss alternative educational opportunities that may get brothers off the streets.

Vocational Schools

I remember pre-integration schools in black communities. My high school had a mixture of educational and vocational classes. We had a dry cleaners, masonry shop, tailoring shop, restaurant, and auto mechanics shop. Many students took advantage of these different trades. There may be a need to return to some aspects of the "old school." The vocational approach allows hands-on approaches to educating our youth, while providing a way to make a living. After the reaction squad has determined that the student will not return to school, admission to a vocational/trade school should be considered.

We must petition our politicians to address more vocational education programs for high school dropouts. Providing young brothers with alternative educational opportunities will inspire more to leave lives of crime, unemployment, and mischief in order to pursue specific trade careers. Attending vocational classes with people their own age prevents the embarrassment of returning to school. The hands-on training will lessen the boredom many experience.

The General Educational Development (GED) Certificate

The GED certificate is a great alternative form of education for those brothers who have dropped out of school and have no intentions of returning.

The American Council on Education has established the following eligibility requirements for GED testing:

- Each state or other jurisdiction administers the GED tests to any qualified adult who resides within that jurisdiction and who meets residency requirements.

- Only persons who do not hold a traditional high school diploma nor have previously earned a GED are eligible to take the GED tests.

- The GED tests are not administered to candidates who are enrolled in an accredited high school, including those accredited by regional accrediting bodies and those approved by jurisdiction department of education.

If none of the above is appropriate for your sons, consider researching other alternatives. You would be surprised at the many available programs that would keep young brothers off the streets!

There is another form of education missing in our communities:

Social Etiquette

We must teach young brothers the proper way to shake hands; we must teach young brothers to be gentlemen; we must teach our young brothers manners; we must teach our young brothers to take their hats off in buildings; and we must teach young brothers how to respect women. Instead of financing bling, designer wear, and expensive sneakers, buy the brother a suit! Teach him how to tie a tie!

Financial Literacy

Our young brothers are being pimped! Media, clothing, jewelry, and shoe corporations are making millions from the purchases of young brothers. They have become major consumers of designer wear, jewelry and tennis shoes. We must teach our sons to save and invest, not buy what they can't afford. We must teach them the importance of establishing and maintaining good credit scores. I have found that many young brothers have keen entrepreneurial abilities; why not encourage them to research starting a business? How about influencing them to finish trade school and start their own businesses? How about a lawn service? What about teaching savings and investments strategies? A statement that I make always catches the attention of my mentees: "It is not what you drive, but what you drive up to (home ownership!)."

Sex Education

Although celibacy should remain at the forefront, we must also stress sex education. Too many young brothers are fathering children from lustful and loveless unions. We must educate them on proper protection and the consequences of unplanned births, sexually transmitted diseases, and HIV/AIDS. Teach the brothers to "wrap it up"!

Learn to Serve

The Corporation for National Community Service has a program entitled Learn and Serve. This program incorporates service learning in college curricula. The students are required to engage in some form of volunteer service. Why not heavily emphasize this approach in our middle and high schools? Young brothers will be involved in community service activities. I am confident they will eventually love engaging those less fortunate or in need. It will positively enhance their attitudes and beliefs.

In reviewing this chapter, let's remember to first develop effective strategies to prevent young brothers from dropping out of school. If the young brother is too far gone and drops out, search for alternative educational opportunities. We must also teach the basics of social etiquette, financial literacy, sex education, and learning to serve.

Notes:

_____

_____

_____

_____

_____

_____

_____

_____

_____

_____

_____

_____

_____

CHAPTER 9

Course of Action #6
Mentor, Mentor, Mentor!

He let me tell my story, and he has been walking with me every day since.
—Tyrone Lynn
Program Manager
Washington, DC

This chapter is important because it deals with the core development of our young brothers. This chapter is devoted to men throughout this country who are: 1) presently successfully mentoring; 2) presently mentoring but getting frustrated; 3) presently mentoring but thinking of severing the relationship; 4) presently entering a mentoring relationship; 5) presently interested in learning more about mentoring; and 6) presently interested in mentoring, but with reservations.

I have experienced all of the above. There are times in one's life that mentoring will not be a priority. There are life challenges, family requirements, and job demands that will sometimes prevent you from mentoring at a certain time. If you find yourself with not enough time, wait until you do have the time. Mentoring is a long-term commitment. Too many of these young brothers have already been disappointed by their fathers' absence or their father or other potential mentors coming in and out of their lives. They are looking for consistency, genuineness, loyalty, and strength. Many have previously let their guards down, resulting in hurt and disappointment. Therefore, initially, you will find a natural barrier to trusting relationships.

You will find that a true measure of establishing trust is hanging in there when these young brothers do not initially respond. I have found that they are observing your reaction to their rejection. These initial fragile relationships will grow into strong ones. In most cases, these young brothers will eventually come around and be talking your heads off, sharing their innermost thoughts and frustrations. Eventually, you will be able to identify the "Red" brothers, those who are so deeply involved in lives of crime or misguided thoughts that they have absolutely no desire to accept help in "pulling their pants up." I recommend, *at least for now*, moving on to a Yellow brother. One day, you will find that the Red brother is ready for help.

This chapter relates to all young brothers, however is most applicable to the sometimes hard to reach Yellow brothers. Please also take nuggets from this chapter in dealing with the Green brothers as well. It is my prayer that this book will inspire and motivate men to either continue mentoring or become mentors. Although frustrating at times, mentoring can be extremely gratifying. It's exhilarating to realize that in some way you have made a major contribution to the positive development of these young brothers. It is like molding clay. You have the power to shape it into a great product. Sure, there will be difficulties. As with molding clay, you sometimes have to start all over again with a different approach.

I want this chapter to provide you help in developing and sustaining trusting relationships. In most cases, you will find that these young brothers have tough exteriors. Remember, projecting toughness is their best survival tactic. However, as you develop trust, you will find that toughness wanes and their vulnerabilities appear. You will discover that when properly developed, these young brothers possess great character. Although they may give the impression that they are not listening, they really are. They will later recite verbatim something you said years before.

You earlier read the willing vessels testimonies in chapter 2. I have decided to address the common threads of these testimonies. Through these common threads, you will learn about their perceptions, first impressions, and other nuggets you can extract to enhance your mentoring skills.

In developing their trust, you must also lower your guard. If you open yourself to them, sharing your victories, frustrations, setbacks, and vulnerabilities, they will feel the relationship is a two-way street. They will also feel more at ease in opening up to you. You will find that the more honest and open you are, the more they will respond accordingly. They will at times see themselves in you.

Case in Point: Willing Vessels' quotes

"I saw something familiar in him, and he cared."

"We have shared many laughs, tears, accomplishments and setbacks together."

"Then I remember asking questions about him, because I was tired of him getting into my business."

"Gil was a lot like me. He didn't back down either."

"I saw so much of myself in him that it was scary."

A friend of mine calls my work with young brothers, social security, for when I get old and need some form of help, they will not hesitate to be there for me. I hope that this private and proud man will never require this type of help, but one never knows. Here we go again with Abdual. He once told me that he "loved me" and would "put diapers on me when I get old." My initial response was quite sarcastic; however, when I thought about it, in his own way, this young brother was expressing the highest form of respect and love. Ironically, the brother that gave me the most hell is now one of my closest friends.

It is now such a great feeling to see these young brothers with their wives and/or children. One of my willing vessels had to remind me that he was now a mature man, therefore, we had to take our relationship to the next level: close friends. Initially, it was hard for me to accept these new relationships, but I eventually learned to enjoy my newfound friends. My new friends and I talk about everything, including job issues, our wives and children, and other matters. They call me when they are about to buy a house, about to witness the birth of their children, or sometimes just for a pep talk. I truly cherish these genuine friendships.

Ironically, this strong and great guy that these brothers talk about is now experiencing a slump in life. Yeah, I know it may be a midlife crisis. However, whatever it is, it doesn't feel good. I feel that I have remained stagnant for the past few years. I oftentimes can't seem to get motivated. I too get frustrated for not living up to my fullest potential ... the very thing I pushed with young brothers. During this period of my life, I have found these young brothers giving me the same advice I once gave them. This is called reverse mentoring—when the mentee now mentors the mentor. Other than my wife, daughter, and a couple of friends, I find myself feeling more comfortable talking to these young brothers than I do most people my age. Just think: these reverse mentors are helping me actualize TIM ... Go figure. Enough about my issues; let's move on to the young brothers.

Please remember that not all of these young brothers walked around with their pants hung low; like mentors, young brothers come in all shapes, sizes, and backgrounds. I would first like to discuss perceptions from these young brothers. I assure you that these are the same perceptions young brothers on the block have today. Let us remember that wrong or right, perceptions are real to the individual who perceives. Therefore, we must be sensitive and knowledgeable of perceptions so that we can adjust our strategies for effective mentoring.

I offer you some quotes from the willing vessels testimonials as they relate to perceptions. Understanding these perceptions will greatly assist in actualizing the "T" in TIM: *trust.*

PERCEPTIONS

"Although I had always been eager to learn, up until then I had never had a true and good example."

"I thought I would never see him much because people his age tend to only show up when it is beneficial to their personal cause."

"So often our young people believe that no one cares if they live or die."

"Most people never step outside of themselves to help the greater masses."

"So often their dreams are deferred because they have no one to help nurture them."

"So often are their cries for help ignored because the older generation doesn't understand the new language of youth—or the generations in between are too focused on "getting paid.""

"I had no idea that I would meet someone who cared about brothers and sisters' well-being."

"Most people his age do not want to be involved with young couples."

"So many others will and have taken my card and never thought about it again."

"In a society where you frequently find phony, self-absorbed, and self-centered "role models" ...""

"I am constantly inspired by the fact that Gil has chosen to serve while many others have turned and run in fear from our young people."

I tend to agree with some of these perceptions. I recall some years ago fussing at a young brother, complaining how selfish his generation was. He replied, and respectfully I must add, "Don't forget that your generation produced my generation." I was speechless because what he said made a lot of sense. Our generation does have to share some responsibility. I recall one brother saying that many of our professional elite are "thugs in suits." The cutthroat, do anything and step on anyone to get ahead approaches are quite similar to the tactics used by brothers on the street. Our generation must ensure that our good talk is followed with good walk.

I for one have noticed that some of my African American male counterparts are so impressed with their accomplishments, and so proud of how far they have come, that they exude a certain arrogance, which is immediately detected by young brothers. Too many look down on young brothers, demanding that they pull themselves up by their bootstraps. I am a firm believer that these well accomplished brothers have been helped and/or mentored in some form or another.

I sense the same arrogance from those who are doing better profession-ally and financially than I am. Calls and e-mails go unanswered; greetings are ignored; and there is even one brother whom I perceive will only shake the hands of those he feels are of a certain status. He is quite nauseating. Yes, some of us have arrived; however, we must realize that America will not totally arrive until the majority of its people from all persuasions have done so as well.

What is so refreshing about young brothers is their raw innocence. They want you to be genuine; they want you to always keep it real with them; they want you not to act as if you are perfect; they want you to tell them the truth; they want you to accept them where they are presently in life; they want you to provide structure; they want you to be accessible; they want you to be who you are; and they want you to hold them accountable.

Too many mentors have failed at mentoring due to their preoccupation with showing young mentees their large houses, luxury cars, expensive jewelry, tailor-made clothes, and their great jobs. Unbelievably, most of the conversa-tion pertained to them rather than the young brother. Some of these mentors then wonder why there was no connection and subsequently blame the young brothers.

Please never think that your job title makes a difference to these young men. They are more concerned with your commitment to the long haul; providing structure and direction lacking in their environments; wanting to know if you have their backs; knowing that you have their best interests at heart. Believe me, they can spot a phony miles away. They don't want someone who just wants to "beef up" their resume helping these poor at-risk youth; they want someone they can trust.

Some of our white brethren think they have to change who they are to com-municate. Some start acting and talking as if they were products of the hood. My best advice to them is to be themselves. There will probably be some com-munication, cultural, and background issues, and they may have to endure some teasing. However, these young brothers will eventually look beyond the color of their skins and accept them as someone they can trust. Once you are knowledgeable of perceptions, you have succeeded in the first step of developing trust. Let's talk about ways to approach our young brothers.

THE APPROACH

Let's now discuss first impressions:

"First thing I thought was, Who is this dude?"

"My first thought was, This guy has balls!"

"My first thought was, this guy is going to be trouble."

"This guy is big, but we really don't need any extras in our conversation."

"When someone told me the loud voice was the colonel's, part of me said, I am getting out of ROTC if he starts tripping."

"Immediately I knew he was a man of distinction, integrity, and character."

"The first thing I thought when I met him was, Whoa! This guy is intense. I don't know if I can take four years of this." I also thought, "I really like him. He seems like someone I can trust."

"He so impressed me that I just had to find out more about this man."

"My first impression of the colonel was that he was going above and beyond to motivate the cadets we had in the program at the time."

"His presence was overpowering, his words were distinct, and actions were distinguished."

"Once in his office, this massively built man stood up to shake my hand, and I quaked just a second."

We all know that first impressions are lasting impressions. The same is true with young brothers. I am now talking about approaching our "Yellow" brothers. I have mastered first impressions. I always leave them intrigued—to the point that they eagerly want another encounter. I recommend you use an approach that you feel comfortable with. I have learned that you want to leave your first session with them wanting to know more about you. Don't be perceived as trying too hard or being too friendly. Get your nerves together before the first encounter. Don't let them see you sweat.

As the young people say, make sure you "come correct." I always address them as sir, young man, young brother, or gentlemen (I recommend to my white brethren not to address them as "young brother"). When you address them correctly, they will eventually give you what I call "that look." I notice it all the time when striking up a conversation with a new young brother. "That look" conveys the following: Are you talking to me? Are you calling me sir? Are you really interested in my well-being? Why would you be interested in what I have to say? In many cases, they are totally surprised that someone is interested in them. Many are caught off guard by the respectful tone. Doesn't that speak volumes?

There are times I see young brothers on the street. I may ask, "How are you young brothers doing?" or "How are you young men doing?" In most cases, they will provide a positive reply. *Never* approach young brothers if you are afraid. They can sense fear, and they immediately believe they have the upper hand. Remember, a strong presence is essential. Look them straight in the eye when you are talking to them; never look down if they give you a mean or long glance. When they see a show of strength, they will reply in kind. Remember, the majority of these young brothers do not have strong male role models.

Learn to use your strengths to your advantage. I am a big guy; therefore, I definitely use it to my advantage. Another advantage I have is my passion—it becomes contagious. You may have the gift for gab, a strong athletic build or acumen, or some other quality that will attract them. Young brothers respect strength and toughness. Again, if you are intimidated or fear for your safety, please *do not* approach them. Find a young brother more your speed.

After the majority of these first encounters, they want to know more about me. They say, "This guys has balls," but they more times than not sense a genuine interest. I think I confuse them because on one hand I come across tough; however, on the other hand, I convey a realistic concern. I recommend you practice with someone you perceive is more your speed and gradually work up.

Don't be concerned if you think you did not connect the first time. In most cases, I leave knowing that I connected. But, in the overwhelming cases that I left thinking I did not connect, I found out later from them that I did. Case in point: most of the aforementioned quotes. Succeeding with a first good impression is your second step in developing trust. You are now well on your way of actualizing TIM.

TRAITS

I would like to highlight some traits that young brothers look for in a potential mentor:

"He never gave up on me."

"And he never backed down along the way."

"If I had to go to battle, he would be the guy I would want backing me up."

"On many occasions, we have squared off with differences of opinion."

"He didn't back down either."

"He was consistent in checking up on me and offering sometimes needed but unwanted advice."

"He just doesn't just talk the talk; he lives it!"

"You see, good people, this is a friend, someone who doesn't always agree with you, but someone who always agrees to listen."

"I thank God for sending a man who was so real and who cared about making a difference in young people's lives."

He has always encouraged me to follow my dreams."

"This is the type of personal character trait he possesses. He would help you, and you would enjoy the help or would not hesitate to listen to his feedback."

"His uncompromising expectation of near perfection was what I needed to push me from being just a good student to being a really great person."

"He has an unsettling ability to quickly assess a person—his integrity, character, and will. He then provides pointed direction, guidance and big-brotherly advice or admonition, if needed."

"He sets a standard that is far above what most young men come into contact with."

"The trust and respect that I have for him is easy because I know that he absolutely has my best interests at heart."

After you are well versed on what perceptions young brothers may have of the older generation, and you have made a good first impression and are knowledgeable of traits that really mean something to these brothers, it is now time to put your victories to action.

Never, ever back down from your values. I think many mentors go awry trying to adapt to young brothers' ways of thinking. Don't forget that your experiences and wisdom make you the teacher, and them the student. As expressed in some of the aforementioned quotes, they respect you more if you keep it real with them. They may disagree with your guidance or advice at the time; however, as you gain trust, they will eventually come around to a more positive way of thinking.

Remember, these young brothers respect structure. They will repeatedly observe you, looking for you to eventually waiver. You are, in most cases, the only real father figure they have had to this point. Always maintain high moral values and walk the talk … They really appreciate that. If you are not in the mentoring game for the long haul, please go sit on the sidelines until you are ready. Mentoring is a serious game of life that requires dedicated and committed players. Young brothers look for consistency. They want to know if they can count on you.

Also, I have learned through trial and error to be careful about wanting to give them money every time they are in a financial pinch. You will end up broke if you are constantly giving them money. Remember, financial challenges will always be present; therefore, you don't want to establish a relationship where you constantly provide them with money. Granted, at times I have taken these brothers to lunch and so forth, and in Abdual's case, once loaned him sixty dollars when he was "shooting kind of bad." Please note from his testimonial in chapter 2 that he does not think it was a loan but that I gave it to him. Never again! Through the years, Abdual has had many financial challenges, but he always survives, and now has learned how to handle his financial affairs in a most responsible manner.

I have also found that mentors should not take themselves too seriously. A good sense of humor is always good. I find sarcasm to help in certain situations. Sometimes they may think you are crazy. Abdual constantly says, "Man, you are a crazy dude." He is always laughing at something I say. At times, talking trash greatly contributes to the bonding experience. I have found that a good number of brothers like to talk trash.

Listening is important on both sides. My wife and daughter call me "The Overtalker." Because of my passion for my point of view, sometimes I have a tendency of talking too much when I should be listening. I have learned to listen more. Many times young brothers know the right thing to do but need confirmation. They have the right solutions but just need someone to listen. Through listening, I have often been pleasantly surprised at their methodical thought processes. One of the biggest compliments comes from one of the quotes: "You see, good people, this is a friend, someone who doesn't always agree with you, but someone who always agrees to listen." Take that, Carolyn and Summer!

I have also learned not to forsake my standards. You will find that once you develop trust and demand high standards, they will rise to the occasion. Too many times, mentors lower their standards, thinking they may be too high. This is almost an insult. You are saying these brothers cannot achieve excellence. Achieving high standards bolsters their self-esteem and confidence, and they are ready to move on to other high standards.

Once you get young brothers talking your head off, you have finally earned their trust. They will want to talk to you all the time. As dean of students and vice president of student affairs, the majority of my time was spent talking to students. The brothers would often just drop by. It would ruffle the feathers of my administrative assistant because it would sometimes throw my schedule out of whack. However, I would always remember that the word "student" was in my job title. It was always about the students, and they knew it.

Now that the T in TIM is actualized, we move to inspire and motivate. In some of the quotes, these young brothers talk about my encouraging words. Still, a mentor must ensure that he doesn't overcompensate with constant praise. Use your praise somewhat sparingly, for when you do offer praise, they will cherish it more and be inspired.

Think of Paula, Randy, and Simon, the judges on *American Idol*. Paula sometimes is what I call too syrupy. Even when the performers are not that good, she offers compliments. Randy is not as complimentary as Paula. I think the performers respond and cherish Simon's feedback most of all because he truly keeps it real. Watch the contestants' reactions just before Simon offers his feedback. They are nervous with anticipation to hear what Simon has to say. You want to build the same relationship with your mentee.

My favorite and most familiar two words are *why not?* When young brothers tell me about their plans—some that many others of my generation would think impossible—my reply to them is always *why not*. This always inspires them. Sometimes they may come up short, but this process teaches them that they can pursue their dreams if they commit and work hard for it. Many times they have come up short, but they always come back to discuss how they can change their approach on the next try. Inspire them to fear not, so they can accomplish their life's desire.

Now that you have inspired, you have actualized the *I* in TIM. Let's now discuss motivation. Once you have developed their trust and inspired them, you will find that motivating them will become less difficult. Your familiarity with these young brothers will allow you to determine the best ways to motivate them.

My motivation techniques may be different from yours. I am known to be quite fussy. Amazingly, the more I fuss, the more they respond. A quote from Abdual's testimony in chapter 2 says, "As time went on, we began to grow close, and from that point forward, he was constantly putting his foot up my butt." He also wrote, "I don't let anyone talk to me the way he does, and no one knows as much about me as he does." Young brothers call and come by for me to fuss at them. They all say it motivates them to do the things they already know they should be doing. Periodically, Abdual will call and say, "Pops, give me some of that negativity." Yes, my negative motivation technique has proven to be quite successful. You would be amazed how some of these tough young brothers would nervously approach my office. They knew if they did not bring their A-game, they would receive my wrath.

ME & ABDUAL

I know that "Me and Abdual" is grammatically incorrect. However, I won't give him the satisfaction of putting his name first. I vaguely remember the day we first met, but I do know that I "came correct." I normally would not have confronted a young brother almost immediately about his gold teeth and gold rings. However, I felt the need to take a chance. I recall his having an entire mouth of gold and a ring on each finger. He of course denies this and says that as I get older, I tend to exaggerate.

The test came when I invited him up to my office. If he said that he had something else to do, I would have known that I went too far too early. I knew that he was intrigued when he followed me to my office. I knew that I had connected. I am known for being able to get someone's life story within the first five to ten minutes of meeting. My assumptions were correct about Abdual. He was from the inner city and had grown up in poverty. He later taught me that the truly tough guys are normally quiet. They don't have to prove they are tough. In retrospect, when I first saw Abdual on the stairs of the Hunter Building, he was minding his own business, just observing his surroundings. However, over the years, I have learned that if people bring drama to him, they will have a lot on their hands!

He left my office rather impressed that a college administrator would take time to sit with him and discuss his background and potential obstacles to his success. We bonded that day. As time passed, our relationship grew stronger.

We got to the point where we would discuss anything. We talked about girls. Abdual is quite the ladies' man. Over the years, we have discussed his need for protected sex. By the way, he was one of those young students I mentioned earlier on the abstinence kick. I don't think Abdual lasted more than a couple of days. Abdual will tell you that he is amazed how well I know him. I can tell when he is lying and will immediately call him out on some things. Like the time he told me that he was abstinent, when I knew full well that he had sex the night before, or said that he had a certain amount of money saved in the bank, when he didn't have a dime. After mentoring for so long, I have almost mastered identifying when they are giving me a load of crap. As trust develops, young brothers will pretty much keep it real with you. If they don't initially, they will eventually fess up because their consciences start bothering them.

One major obstacle to Abdual's journey was finances. Although he would earn money, he could never tell me where it went. We have even sat down and literally gone over where the money went. He could never give me a full account. We would discuss why he always felt the need to have a big, fancy car.

I think it made him feel good about himself. What I tried to teach him to do was stop wanting short-term pleasure and prepare for long-term gain. Abdual has finally transformed from a constant consumer to a saver and investor. He recently bought his first house. It is a three-bedroom, two-bath, two-car garage home on almost an acre. A few weeks later, he gave me a complete tour of his new home. He was proud, and so was I. He has started his own company, JerZ Media Productions, and is doing quite well. Guess what? This proud homeowner now drives a "hoopty."

My journey with Abdual has enhanced my mentoring skills. I have learned that a mentor cannot take things too personally. Although you want the best for your mentee, you may find yourself taking the problem or issue more seriously than they do. At times, I would get more stressed than they did. I have learned that after counseling them, let them carry their own burden. Sometimes their good decisions lessen or alleviate the burden, and bad decisions make the burden heavier. They learn best this way. They must determine how long they are going to carry the burden.

At times, I would get so upset with Abdual that I would say, "The hell with him." Through my life's experiences, I was often able to point out potential pitfalls; however, he would go and fall into the very pit I warned about. One thing about Abdual: after he fell into the pit and dug himself out, he would always man up and come back to me saying that he should have listened. Over the years, this has happened countless times. At least he knew I would always be there when he needed to talk things out. Lord, I have been there for him through his many trials, tribulations, and errors—most of the time only listening. I also eventually learned not to constantly say, "I told you so." Of course, I had to tell him that at least once, and then we would move forward, dissecting where he went wrong. I was always amazed how this very bright young brother could pinpoint exactly where he went wrong.

Sometimes I would see great progress with Abdual, and sometimes I'd see the same old behavior. I would go home to Carolyn saying that I was going to cut Abdual loose. In fact, many times I would say the same about other mentees. She would always give me a look that said, "You know that you are not going to give up on this young brother."

Abdual now has two children. He is truly a great father, and his daughter and son are the loves of his life. We discuss his plans for his kids' futures. He recently sent me a picture of him and his kids. Both look just like him. If you come into my office, you will see a collage of many young brothers and their families. They proudly send me pictures, and I proudly display them.

Abdual has helped me enhance my street smarts. He will sometimes warn me about people, telling me to be careful about this person or that person. In most cases, he has been right. I would ask him how he rightly predicted how these people were. His reply: "Game knows game."

Although over the years I have been very hard on Abdual, he has never, ever disrespected me (nor have any of the scores of other mentees). I must admit, as he gets older and acts more responsibly, I am not fussing as much (I kind of miss the fussing). We are now two men who are close friends. Abdual is the son Carolyn and I never had. He also gets along with Summer, as if he were her brother. I catch him looking at me sometimes as if to say, "Dean is really getting old." I was forty-two when we met, and now I am fifty-three. As I have seen Abdual grow older, he has also seen me do the same.

The other day, he was asking how I was coming with the book and my business. I told him that it was a little behind. He called me a slacker. I did not like that, however, through his negativity, I became more motivated. I guess I should start calling him periodically, saying, "Abdual, give me some of that negativity." I guess my "son" is a chip off the old block. I know Abdual won't ever let me forget my next sentence. But, I really can't imagine Abdual not being in my life. There, I said it. My plan is to have Me & Abdual mentoring workshops throughout the country. I told him about this plan and his response was, "I am ready Pops!"

My best words of advice for effective mentoring:

- Come correct.
- Show a genuine interest in their well-being.
- Always keep it real.
- Share your frustrations, issues, etc. with them, resulting in two-way communication.
- Never back down from your principles.
- Listen to their issues and help them devise a plan.
- If they fail, help them dissect where they went wrong.
- Listen to them and allow them to talk out their own solutions.
- Be there whenever they call upon you; have their backs even when you are telling them they are dead wrong!
- Help them develop a TIMplate for life!

Notes on Common Threads and Mentoring:

_____

_____

_____

_____

_____

_____

_____

_____

_____

_____

_____

_____

_____

_____

_____

_____

_____

CHAPTER 10

Course of Action #7
Develop a TIMplate for Life!
By Carolyn Knowles

May He give you the desire of your heart and make all your plans succeed.
Psalm 20: 4
(Holy Bible, NIV)

When you begin to develop a rather good relationship with your mentee, I strongly recommend using the TIMplate. You often have to guide young brothers in the life plan process. Initially, it may seem painful to sit down with them and get them to talk about what they want out of life. I think you will find using the TIMplate quite useful in better understanding the young brother's innermost thoughts. This will definitely facilitate the actualization of TIM. A script is also provided for this process:

Have you thought about what you want to be in life? Where you want to go? What you want to do? Have you considered how you want to be remembered by your children, parents, relatives, friends, and community? Will the world be better because you passed through?

As an African American male living in times like these, it is recommended that you develop a life plan. Statistics reveal that you may have a shorter life span than those from other ethnic groups. However, do not speak such negativity on yourself. It may seem as if many brothers around you are dying, but only speak blessings on your life. Know that you were made for a purpose, and that your life has value. However, it is up to you to discover the talents, gifts, and abilities that lie within. You must discover who you are.

This section is devoted to young men who may or may not be at risk, as well as mentors, teachers, and youth advocates. It presents a script that can be used to walk through the development of a life plan, along with a TIMplate for Life, which serves as a tool to assist in the process.

Who am I?

Choose to take a unique approach in determining who you are. Instead of identifying your parents, siblings, and other family members; your birth date and birthplace; or even your education level, I recommend you start by conducting an "I am" exercise. This requires you to choose at least five adjectives that describe you. Then you are to write a short paragraph that explains why you are embodied in that description. Examples are shown below:

> I Am–Blessed

> I am blessed because I have love, joy, and peace in my life. They reside inside of me and come out of me, as I interact with and impact the lives of those around me.

> I Am—Healthy

> I woke up this morning with a sound mind. I am able to think, see, and smell. I am able to taste, hear, and move around. I can smile, and I can laugh. I can choose to be happy or choose to be sad.

> I Am–Handsome

> When I look into the mirror, what do I see? I see my reflection looking right back at me. I see a handsome and vibrant man, with hope for a future that leads me to success.

> I Am–Wise

> I have good judgment and a spirit of discernment. I know when I am right, and I know when I am wrong. It is my goal to follow that wisdom in all of my thoughts, words, and deeds.

> I Am—Honest

> I do believe that honesty is the best policy. No matter what situation I am in, I will be true to myself, to others, and to God.

These five examples focus on the positive self. I implore you to speak blessings on your life. Do not allow the power of your tongue to curse your life. Remember ... you are determining who you are.

What is my status?

The next step is to accept who you are and determine your status. I decided to surf the Internet for a definition of the word "status." Wikipedia defines status as a state, condition, or situation. This leads me to encourage you to address several aspects of your status. Where are you right now in terms of spiritual, physical, emotional, financial, professional, and social well-being?

- Spiritual

  Seek to communicate with your inner spirit. This requires you to spend time with yourself in thought and/or meditation. You may find yourself believing in a higher being. This relationship can help you through this journey called life. A good spiritual foundation can promote sanity in an insane world. It can keep you rooted in those things that are positive and worthy of emulation.

- Physical

  Remind yourself regularly that your body is your temple. If you expect it to be healthy, then you must properly care for and maintain it. Be conscious of the things you allow to enter it, and be aware of the places you take it. Good nutrition and exercise, proper rest and relaxation, regular medical checkups, and safety practices can contribute to good physical health.

- Emotional

  There are many stressors in life that can send you on an emotional roller coaster if you are not careful. Many of these feelings are normal … but many can become harmful. For example, to love and be loved is a good feeling. However, when that love is one-sided, you may feel emotions such as rejection, unworthiness, and/or anger. These negative emotions can be harmful if they are not properly controlled. In these times, having a strong spiritual foundation can positively impact your thoughts and your actions. That inner spirit can remind you that though tears may last for a night, joy often comes in the morning.

- Financial

  Do you earn an income from a job? Or do you receive an allowance from parents and/or caregivers? Do you budget how that money is spent? If so, I commend you. If not, I recommend you develop a financial plan that addresses spending, saving, and investing. Otherwise, you can easily be motivated and manipulated to spend continuously. And sometimes you may not even realize just how much you have spent. You may then begin to think that you need to earn more money. I suggest you monitor your dollars and cents to determine if you may instead be spending too much money. A financial plan can help you track what comes in your treasure chest and what goes out.

A point of caution is the excessive use of credit. It can be one of your financial tools, but you must practice discipline in using it. I suggest that you think about a purchase before making it. Use cash instead of credit when you can. You will be amazed how much less you spend when you actually use your own cash. Don't get caught up in the "credit nightmare." Doing so can bring undue hardship and stress into your life.

Use your financial plan to empower yourself. Identify those strengths and areas for improvement and then launch your path toward financial well-being.

- Professional

Are you in a job or career that you enjoy? You may wonder if there is a difference between a job and a career. For our purposes, a job is work performed in exchange for payment. It can be your trade, occupation, or profession. On the other hand, a career is typically an area that you are trained in, and one that you consider a permanent calling.

You may have several jobs before you choose a career ... and that's okay. The question that begs an answer is, "What are your expectations?" Can your job or career satisfy your professional expectations? Are you passionate about what you are doing, or are you just in it for the paycheck? Either way, I suggest you reflect on what's important to you. Do you want to make a lot of money? Or do you just want to be happy? Or do you want both? Whatever you decide, remember that typically the difference between a job and a career deals with education and training. You must make proper preparations to realize your dreams.

- Social

All work and no play can lead to a boring and unfulfilling life. Take time to be social. Establish relationships. Have lots of fun. The only precaution I suggest is ensuring that you surround yourself with positive people who are doing positive things. Together you can impact your personal lives and your communities in a strong social way.

What are my goals and objectives?

After you have determined your status, the next step is to identify your short-term and long-term goals and objectives. Use the same categories as above to determine where you want to be. I suggest that you list specific thoughts, ideas, concepts, timelines, and costs. Be a visionary and keep the vision alive. Be a dreamer and expect abundance. But most of all, remember to write down the plan and make it clear. Also, revisit, revise, and renew the plan along the way.

By identifying your goals and objectives, you have demonstrated your interest in your personal growth. Please understand that personal growth is a continuous process that involves lifelong learning. I encourage you to aim high, stay focused, and expect great success.

What do I like doing?

Do you like reading, watching television, or surfing the Net? Do you like jogging, dancing, or playing sports? Do you prefer to be inside or outside? Do you prefer to be around people or spend your downtime alone? By answering these questions, you can determine what your hobbies are or could be. The key is to have a hobby and to pursue it actively.

Not everything has to be a hobby. Several other areas might attract your interest. Examples may include things like viewing art, wine tasting, or even traveling domestically and/or abroad. The key is to acknowledge those things that capture your attention. At some point in your life, you may have the opportunity to partake of them, and they may move from the area of interest to the area of hobby.

There are twenty-four hours in a day. For most people, a large percentage of these hours are spent sleeping and working. For our purpose, let's say eight hours are spent sleeping and eight hours are spent working. How do you spend the remaining eight hours? Another exercise I recommend is called "OTT—Other Time Takers." Over a period of a seven-day week, determine how you spend your free time. Are you doing things for others, for yourself, or for everybody? Are you tired and stressed out, or are you rested and at peace? Doing this exercise helps you identify those things in your life that are important and those things that are not. It also allows you to see if you are being reactive or proactive. Is there always an urgent situation that befalls you? If so, I suggest you reflect on and reevaluate how you will spend your time.

In these days, it is critical to have good time management skills. Otherwise, you will find yourself in a constant state of stress and frustration. This can lead to sickness and pain that is preventable.

By now, you have identified hobbies, interests, and other time takers. Is it possible that your passion exists within one of these areas? I suggest you make time to further define and reflect on your passions. Seek to pursue the dreams and desires placed in your heart, for one of those may be your divine destiny. Your passion promotes excitement and devotion to an activity that you would love doing even if you were not paid.

What do I do well?

You have knowledge, skills, and abilities that directly impact the types of jobs you hold or the career you choose to pursue. You may be a white-collar worker or you may be a blue-collar worker. You may have that entrepreneurial spirit, wherein you are your own boss. Many young brothers have started small businesses, such as yard cutting, mailbox painting, car washing, and so on. It does not matter what category you are in. What matters is that practice makes perfect. The more you hone your skills, the better you become.

You have talents and gifts that are yours to discover and execute. Are you a talented singer, dancer, or athlete? Are you a gifted comedian, designer, or photographer? Are you working in your spiritual gifts? You may have the gift of encouragement, discernment, teaching, or something else. The bottom line is to determine what you do well … and do it.

Another approach is to identify your strengths and your strengths in progress (same as areas for improvement). For example, you may have strong writing skills. However, while you are updating those skills through seminars, workshops, and courses, they are strengths in progress.

What do I have experience doing?

You may know how to use a computer, but are you a novice or are you an information technology specialist? There are basic, moderate, and expert levels of experience in any field. I suggest you identify those areas where you have experience and further determine the level you are at. You may be able to broaden that expertise through additional training and/or education. For example, if you have military experience, whether as an enlisted person or as an officer, you may have had the opportunity to conduct training. Once you depart the military, that experience may be further developed by obtaining a certificate or degree, which could launch your career in that field.

What are my guiding principles?

Ethics, morals, and values play a significant role in behavior. What's inside of you will come out of you ... and what comes out of you affects all who are around you. Therefore, it is especially necessary to have a set of guiding principles for your life.

There are now four generations in the workplace: Traditionalists—born 1900–1945; Baby Boomers—born 1946–1964; Generation X—born 1965–1980; and Generation Y—born 1981–2000.[5] These groups bring much diversity into the workplace. Each has its core values and beliefs. However, each must find a way to coexist and thrive in today's economy.

There are several sources available to provide guidance on how you should live, work, and play. Specifically, there is the Bible, with its Ten Commandments; other religious books, with ethical and moral principles outlined; corporate standard operating procedures for behavior in the workplace; and rules, laws, and regulations for society as a whole. No matter what the source, the bottom line is that you need guiding principles for your life.

What do I want my legacy to be?

As you have realized, the purpose of this section is to have you focus on developing a life plan that works for you. Does writing the plan down mean automatic success? No, I cannot guarantee that. However, I can guarantee that a life plan, which is written, revisited, revised, and renewed as needed, will allow you to be more organized. It will help you to know where you are, where you want to go, and how you want to get there.

Your knowledge, skills, and abilities, along with your talents and gifts, make you a unique person. As a final task, choose to write your autobiography, which is your personal account of your life. What will be said about you? Did you make a difference in your family, community, your country, or the world? Did you keep your vision alive? Did you dream big dreams? Did you act on those dreams? Is the world better because you passed through?[4]

---

5   Gallup Research

Use the TIMplate for Life as a tool to assist you in getting started. Let this be a journey of self-love, self-discipline, and self-motivation. Stay positive. Practice turning weaknesses into areas for improvement or strengths in progress. Seek support from family, relatives, friends, mentors, teachers, preachers, and other youth advocates.

Commit to the Lord whatever you do, and your plans will succeed.

Proverbs 16:3
(Holy Bible, NIV)

TIMplate for Life

TRUST ♦ INSPIRE ♦ MOTIVATE

Help Them Pull Their Pants Up includes this TIMplate, which is designed as a tool for mentors to use in guiding mentees through self-assessment and development of a life plan. While this TIMplate cannot guarantee success, it can help mentors and mentees to bond and develop the trust factor as they share important dreams, visions, values, concepts, and philosophies of life.

The TIMplate should be a formal part of the mentoring process. It should be introduced after the first or second meeting. Approximately thirty minutes should be allowed for a face-to-face discussion on what the TIMplate is, and how it can be used in the mentoring relationship. Afterward, the mentee should be given one week to reflect upon the critical questions and concepts therein. During the following week, the mentor and mentee should begin to write the plan down.

A formal session should be scheduled to discuss the mentee's written plan. Upon completion of that session, the mentee should sign the plan and commit to revisit, revise, and renew it as needed. The mentee should put this TIMplate in a place where it is easily accessible and readily available. The mentor should plan to hold the mentee accountable by requesting periodic updates.

During the initial stages of mentoring, the trust factor is being developed. It is critical to have a definition of a mentor that the mentee understands and accepts. It might even be beneficial to let the mentee know what a mentor is not. Ensure that there are proper expectations of the relationship.

Once trust is established, the mentor has an opportunity to "inspire" and "motivate" the mentee through personal example and facilitation of growth experiences in the mentee's spiritual, physical, emotional, financial, professional, and social life. Use this TIMplate and get started today. Remember, it is only a guide, and each mentor can determine his approach and/or technique while walking through this process.

KNOWLESwhattodoTIMplate

A tool for mentors to guide mentees through self-assessment and development of a life plan

Life Plan

I. Who Am I?

    a. Conduct an "I am" exercise, choosing at least five adjectives that describe me. Write a short paragraph that explains why I am embodied in that description.

    b. Reflect on my blessings, focusing on those things for which I am thankful.

II. What Is My Current Status?

    a. Spiritual–Do I currently seek to communicate with my inner spirit?

    b. Physical–Do I remind myself that my body is my temple?

    c. Emotional–Am I currently aware of those things that lead to stress?

    d. Financial–Do I have a financial plan?

    e. Professional–Am I preparing to have a career? Or am I deciding to accept jobs throughout my life?

    f. Social–Do I have positive social relationships?

III. What Are My Short-Term Goals and Objectives?

    a. Spiritual–What will I do immediately to seek to communicate with my inner spirit?

b. Physical–What behaviors will I immediately identify and adopt to promote good health? How often will I remind myself that my body is my temple?

c. Emotional–What are some of the potential stressors in my life? How will I overcome them?

d. Financial–What are some things I can do to improve my short-term financial situation?

e. Professional–What are my plans for education and training? How will my skill level impact my way of making a living?

f. Social–How can I improve and/or expand my positive social relationships?

IV. What Are My Long-Term Goals and Objectives?

a. Spiritual–How will I ensure a long-term relationship with my inner spirit?

b. Physical–What can I do to be fit for life?

c. Emotional–What can I do to promote lifelong emotional health?

d. Financial—How can I empower myself through financial stability/security?

e. Professional–What are some expected outcomes from the career I choose?

f. Social–What are some of the benefits I can receive from having strong and positive social relationships throughout my life?

V. What Do I Like Doing?

a. Hobbies–Do I have a hobby? If so, do I actively pursue it? If not, why not?

b. Interests–Do I acknowledge those things that capture my attention? If so, write them down. If not, start noticing them and write them down.

c. Other Time Takers (OTTs)–Conduct an "OTT" exercise, where I identify other time takers in my life and write them down.

VI. What Do I Do Well

a. Talent(s)–Identify my talent(s).

b. Gifts(s)–Identify my spiritual gift(s).

    c.   Strengths–What areas am I strong in?

    d.   Strengths in Progress–What are some areas I am working to improve upon?

VII. What Do I Have Experience Doing?

    a.   Basic Level–Do I have minimum experience in any particular area?

    b.   Moderate Level–Do I have a fair amount of experience in any particular area?

    c.   Expert Level–Do I have experience that qualifies me as an expert in any particular area?

VIII. What Are My Guiding Principles?

    a.   Ethics–How do I determine what is good and what is bad?

    b.   Morals–How do my morals affect my attitude and behavior?

    c.   Values–How do I determine what is important to me?

IX. What Do I Want My Legacy to Be? Reflect on my personalized TIMplate and be true to myself as I write my own story.

I promise to complete this TIMplate for Life and review, revise, and renew it periodically.

_____   _____

     Signature of mentee   Date

EPILOGUE

I pray that you have enjoyed and learned from this book. There is no doubt that young African American males face great challenges. The fact that these young men are Americans makes it an American challenge—a challenge that has evolved into a tragedy. Ignoring this tragedy now, will only feed it, causing it to grow larger and become more destructive for future generations.

Although some of us may presently live in sanitized environments, thinking that this tragedy does not affect us, it will eventually touch our lives in one way or another. We cannot escape the aftershock of this societal earthquake. If we continually focus on the late-night breaking news, negative statistics, low-hanging pants, and personal prejudices, we will miss opportunities to collectively solve one of America's greatest tragedies.

Please don't paint young African American males with one broad stroke of the brush, for they are as diverse as America's melting pot. Don't forget the many young brothers who have overcome odds that the majority of our white brethren will never experience. Many of them have made lemonade out of lemons; turned rags into fine linen; and, against astronomical odds, achieved the true essence of the American dream.

Too many of these young brothers are living an American nightmare, surrounded by poverty, lack of education, and lack of proper parenting and role modeling. In many cases, they are forced to raise themselves. Children obviously can't effectively raise children. Therefore, adult intervention is required. We must wake these children from their nightmares, so that they can go forward and achieve great and wondrous things.

I beseech all Americans to address this tragedy through tolerance, empathy, and mentorship. I also request that Americans fight our own war against poverty, ignorance, and despair. I am totally convinced that with proper education, mentorship, exposure, and a helping hand, we can defeat the enemies devouring too many of America's youth. Parents, families, mentors, communities, and public officials alike must step up their games.

111

In mentoring these young men, please consider actualizing TIM. Developing and nurturing their trust, inspiring them to reach for the stars, and motivating them to actualize their dreams, will significantly contribute to eliminating this American tragedy. Together, America can successfully *Help Them Pull Their Pants Up*!

Printed in the United States
124993LV00006B/29/P